every lines other

The Collected Poems of Lyx Ish

aka Elizabeth Was

every lines other

The Collected Poems of Lyx Ish
aka Elizabeth Was

preface by Maria Damon

2016

Xexoxial Editions
West Lima, Wisconsin

Designed & edited by mIEKAL aND.
Cover by LiaizonWakest.
Special thanks to Ben Meyers & Maria Damon.

ISBN-10 1-93668-702-X
ISBN-13 978-1-93668-702-2

published by

Xexoxial Editions
10375 County Highway Alphabet
La Farge, WI 54639

perspicacity@xexoxial.org
www.xexoxial.org

Elyxir of Text

A Preface to the Collected Poems of Lyx Ish

by Maria Damon

"I think that I am leaving myself a body of language."

In all registers of life, as she transitioned from Elizabeth Perl Nasaw to Liz Was to Lyx Ish, the writer of the works assembled here strove for liberation, primarily of the imagination in its myriad manifestations, but also freedom from enslavement to exploitive economic systems, sexist body politics and domestic arrangements–ultimately, freedom from a separate self, and freedom to play with the unknown. But over and beyond that, she embodied that goal, which is more properly a process, for the many others she included in her vast raying-out of warmth and influence. The other great and related theme is relationality itself, which is the freedom from separateness: the "bean being bean" that is also being earth, water, air and heat(fire). Her writings, collected here by loving survivors mIEKAL aND and Liaizon Wakest, sparkle with the interplay of her many primal roles: artist, mother, lover, daughter, friend–a "woman" and multi-artist in constant multilogue with those categories–in language that romps and tumbles over itself in gleeful fulfillment of utopian (or, as she writes, "oputian," acknowledging the never-perfect, ever-mutable nature of attempted utopias) intimations.

For this body of writing and writing body, writing=drawing=architecture=sex= dance=music=eating=conversation=exploration=living in a curving continuum of exchange and interbeing; daily social activities are not divided from aesthetic pursuits. Every interaction can be poetic, and every writing is an act of social cultivation. Terror and trauma is addressed but also turned into life-giving adventure and further exploration of experience. In 1983, as she rode her bicycle through the streets of Madison, she was hit by a train and thrown x feet. In a body cast for many months, she had to develop a new relationship to her previously invincible body. There are references to this life-changing event scattered throughout the book in almost every poem: in "Pinkshot," the poem that opens the book, the very first stanza announces her shiny-ball self taken by surprise to be both "inured" and "injured" (in reverse order) by the nonstop train. Years later she gives birth to a son, Liaizon Wakest, known less formally as Zon: knowing that this profound experience will change her relationship to her body as much as the earlier near-death trauma did, she writes: "A trainful of liaisons approach endarchy" (60). "It was the train hit me, everywhere between my cunt and my heart," she writes also, acknowledging exactly the places of love, sex, conception and birth. The "mummy" of the body cast becomes, through a still-embraced sexuality ("I swim foreplay"), somebody's mommy, as she is her own mommy (the word "nascent" is a particular favorite, appearing most dramatically in the piece "I Come from the Nascent Bean," which plays with the charming fictional hipster girlchild Suzuki Beane) and she has a mom, Beatrice, whose name is punned on again and again, a source of Bea-ing. These states of nascence, trapture and emergence are mediated by the figure of the turtle, which became Lyx's emblematic animal (after the articulated movements of the body cast, which both enabled healing and inhibited easy, unself-conscious movement in a "machine-chest choked hegemony"); for an extroverted, exuberant energy like hers, turtledom(e) provided a means of escape into interiority without sacrificing a magnificently ornate, visually complex exterior.

"Who IS the voice that here is a sentence that sings…"

What is an "I"? Lyx asks repeatedly. The "I" is nothing except in relation. "I'm: fishing for the self," but also "I am and opening," not a fixed identity or even a demarcated entity. "Pinkshot/ outside the covet/ of biography." Zippy girlperson escapes the jealous clutches of a narrow biographical index into the wider terrains of bios and graphy: life itself and writing itself, indivisible and intertwined, interdependent. There may be an "I," but it is a member of the alphabet and hence a part of nature and a fiction:

> it is I
> i of the island
> i of the oceans
> i of the tapping words
> …
> tell us a stoooory

To counterbalance the tightly protective turtle, the onion (anagram for "no I, no!") emerges as a potent figure for unleaving, divesting, delving, shuffling off dying self-coils that no longer fit, leaving and unleaving: book leaves, pages, layers of the self and of somatic awareness, leaving New York for Wisconsin, eventually leaving that last mortality coil for an even better unknown. "Onion Leaves, her Map Untended" traces these un/earthings and emergences, these comings and goings. "Parentheses remind her of onion leaves" protecting (but softly and disposably) a sotto voce truth-murmur. The natural world is a written language: Lyx embodied an ecopoetics, re-membering herself through exercising her abilities in all directions. "Is this leaf an onion's remembering[?]"

> *"... & that eye is no organ in clusters parading, out of time, POLYMETER, capitals blacker than some, stances or stanzas in groups of others."*

Lyx's musicianship provided still more figuration for the complexity of the interdependent, expressive self that is no-self. "Hoketus a ladder" is both nominal and verbal: musicians who, strictly forbidding personal expression, riff off each other in discordant but interlocking and improvised trade-offs that create thick interstices of human and instrumental sound, create a means to ascend beyond the self into soundworld; words are these musicians, "lugging ... at the tongue ... letting the same things sing/together in and out/in and out their/surrendering cloud." Breathing music as part of a dissonant collectivity, the "I" is obliterated in breakthrough rather than breakdown. "Victoria and Melampus," a fable about a princess who becomes a bohemian sex goddess, tells of being awakened to herself by a "fascinating café goatboy" who reminds her of many arts both esoteric and common–"painting, writing, yoga, astrology, magic, ritual, taste, reading, &, most scrumptiously, music." This eroticized aesthetic passion for outlying humanist traditions suffuses the writing with "creative skin energy" of the sensate body enjoying its own thinkingfeeling. And again, it's the *freedom* of this new kind of music that sends her rather than the formality of her early training. "Whatever is made stays, but music glides in all directionals."

The eros of art, embodied in this volume's writing, delights in slippages: parts of speech for body parts, propositions for prepositions, metaphors asking comparisons to dance, and "the edge of the sentence connected by little words and their children." "Every Lines Other," among many, many other things an homage to Gertrude Stein (the Stein who wrote "in the midst of merriment there is writing"), is the central piece, the masterwork in several parts and written over the course of a decade. Here given pride of place and framed by the shorter pieces, it is a gleeful feminifesto of the writing body/"bodee"/ bodhi (awakened one), a placement of herself in a tradition of women besotted with art and language and everything else, refusing the minoritarian shame foisted on her by social convention. Like the experiments of Bernadette Mayer in which the detritus and drift of everyday domestic life permeate the fluid body of the poem which is also a daily record of lived life, Every Lines Other is an all-encompassing structure like a house that is a shrine to the sacredness of quotidian, DIY life. People with their complex relationships, friends keeping secrets or lovers both ardent and reserved, children learning to speak, food and its loving preparation, art emerging from the twists and turns of every sound and staircase and texture, are encoded in letters (of the alphabet, in the mail), lines (of the face, the palm, the page, the song, the building), sheets (of music, of beds, of pages, of rain), the body-calligraphy of yoga, punctuation ("…" (ellipsis) as a visual pun on "Liz Was" and "Lyx Ish," commas as come-ons, etc.). The pressure of being trapped in an "I" ("I isolate further my nearest in her fancies") cedes to the aliveness of every human formation, even/especially in extremis: "How people in excruciating transition look so alive"), and all is wound through with this supple, flamboyant skein of language.

"Every Lines Other" is a transposition ("every other line"), and a description: "Every" (individuated subjectivity infinitely multiplied and inclusive) lines, as a sheath or protective inner fabric, the many "Other"s within and around us. The vagina (L. sheath or lining) lines the Other, the (s)word of writing on one's insides; the birth canal protects the birthee by its muscular flexibility and self-lubricating super-powers; Everygirl limns (lines) her world in defamiliarized but intimate resonance.

Though her "Formula for Labor," a clairaudiently channeled chant for childbirth, spells out "A u s c h w i t z" in acknowledgement of the dangers to which she's exposing her emerging child, the vast preponderance of the book spells riotously joyful embrace of the jewomanishly lineage of which she is a quiveringly alive arrow, electrical instance.

This book is liquid, tender, tendriled, polyvalent, sharp, and forever. Drink this text.

Elizabeth Perl Nasaw changed her name to Liz Was when she entered into a long artistic and domestic partnership with mIEKAL aND in 1980, and changed her name again in the late 1990s when she developed an independent creative practice and felt the need for a new identity to match it.

pinkshot

(1984)

shiny ball doesn't stop to think
which town does this train stop
in fast the time or little or no
the time to step and think inured
injured by clench worry be then

wrist dancing the keys red
white fire and wet sees past
and she——
one blind leg
standing on an ocean

i——said the woman on
the bench staring house
one seed in the pit of her
pocket——an opening straight
through to the time before
SHINY BALL DANCING STREET

one page flies over
an electric biography
wandering legs changing
direction together
just today widened
the dot on the
i CAN avail

her other sizes ringing
clang can bumping
red organs hanging
split over a branch
of the way up

we know and we sing
words
slant
repeat
reappeat
synculture
autobeginnings
us
hoketus a ladder
for the midst of things

lugging words at the tongue
pretending under the table
letting same things sing
together in and out
in and out their
surrendering cloud

ONE PAST LIFE IN PARTICULAR
ASKS ME TO REMEMBER SO WE CAN
BE OF NO MIND NEXT TIME

it is i
i of the island
i of the oceans
i of the tapping words
i ring i slander
we know the words
tell us a stoooory

(her strength is thickening
whiter turning pink
she takes too
whose going is taken
as giving which being
she wanders
skin bends pink
from her token
"run the mill
close to her"
insides

forget
there
changing
——

*

i
am
and
opening

TEA LADY CHANTS KABOOM KABOOM
AND FORGETS THE TALKING

MIND DOUBLED ON A HOT BEAT
THE TRAIL HOMEWORD INTO OBLIGATO

EACH SPROUT FUDGE FOR TOMORROWS
BACK WORDS TO THE COMPLISHED TRUNK

THE TOES ARE POWERFUL DISCONNECTION
RETURN LATER TO THE UPRIGHT CIRCLES

DIZZY GIRL IS WINDING UP FOR TAKEOFFS
DISPLACES AIR FOR ARMS WINGS FOR WILL

SLIPS ON WET CITY HISTORY
        COUGHS INTO THE ONLY PHONE
        LEFT RINGING ON EARTH

"THE TIME I GO IS THE SKY
DROPPING ABOVE WITH MUSIC"

HER BATHER EE
  DA HEDD
  DAS GUTE
SIG EN TROENVA

THE LAEFT HANDED WOMAN
FINGERS A SONG ON THE AIR
NO LESION PLANNED
OR MELODIC MODE

GRAPHITE TUNED
TO THE COLOR OF RIVER
CHOIR SITS
FOR A LAMPLIGHTS SUN

SOUND SHUTTERS IN
CLOUD OF MOTION
PARKED BY CHAIRS
BUILDING FOOD
TOO FULL OVER
THE ROCK SED

“DRAM DRAM JAPADI KRONOS”
WORDS RINGING FIT TO BLOW
THE BIG LIFE BIG SCIENCE BIG
TALKING SQUARE BAG OF SEAMS
AND OTHER IN BETWEENS

PISTON AND RITUAL
PINPOINTED RAISON
BRIGHT DEMASSTIC WORKING
“EVERBODY SOUNDS LIKE”
LIGHT FLAILING INTENTION

FUGITIVE OF CLARITY:
CLEAR IN A DREAM
CLEAR IN EMBRACE
CLEARLY UPRIGHT
ZIGZAG FLYER

WOMAN SEARCHING LAYERS
IN A STRAIGHT LINES
IN UNFURNISHED CIRCLES

GIRL HOPPING BUSHES
UNDER BODEES
FRAYING PAINTINGS

JOINTS FOR LOOSELY
TENDERED AFFECTIONS
SPANCE ENTER WINGSPACE

“ITS ANOTHER LOVELY WAYWARD”
ROWS OF VAGRANCE
VING, DRIBBLE, WAP——

"CONNECTIONS ARE FORDERING EXTREMES"
LANGUA ALPHA NORA MANTRA
SPEK TO A WORD ORDER LAUGHING

WHO KNOWS WHEN THE RAMBLING
WRITER CHANGES DIRECTION OR
GOES OUT THE COMMERCIAL TOXIC

VIEWING CRAGGY BOUND SAUNTERINGS
TO THE TUNE OF AN OLIVE TREE
ALL THINGS GIVE EYE
THE EAVES TO AMBLE

DOUBLE THE ALPHA
LET SQUEEZE THE PEN

THE JUNK MAN ROUND MIDNIGHT
TINKERING KEYS
WHITE LINE
RED SPHERE
EYES CLOSED
FINGER TAPPING
HE LISTENS IN ON
SOUNDS BUSSING OWN HALLS

FULL MOUTH MEALY MIND WAITING
IN SELF-CIRCULAR SURRENDER
THERE GOES PEN SOUND WITH FULL
ROUND PERCUSSIVE ANALOGY

THE GOING GOING BODEE ANALEASE
A STOP PADDED BOUNCE OFF DEJECTION
HISTORIC APPRECIATION ROOM WRITING

ZONE TO WANDER IN CLOSED OTHER, SELF?

THE BRIDGE OVER MIND
IS SOUND AN APEX
LEAN INTO WORDS TAP TAP COMPLETE
THOT RUN ONE WAY
CONCEPT ANOTHER SOUND
SUCK AND PET THE MEMORY
MACHINE TO PURR RESULTS

JUNK MAN JA JA JA
O JAR MON BEARING

IT'S TOO LATE TO CAPSULIZE
THE MECHANICS OF THE DREAM
GIVE ME YOUR TAKEN LOT
MUCH TAKEN WORD PEN O PEN

BETTER THE SOFT MAN
GONE AND RISE THEN
SOFT IN LEANING PRONE

"HOME BOMB WRITING DIVE":
CLEAR FILED MIRROR
CITYSCAPE ROUTE
THE SERIOUS MAN GONE
TO FUTURE INNARDS
KWOBE WOMAN TWICE
TRYING EMPTY KNOT
MACHINE LADY
ZEN AS PEKING

LEAPT AND GONE ON
FUTURE EXCURSIONS
BACKWARPS AND AWAY
SILENT DOMINO FIGBATTLE
INTERFERENCE OR LOUD
QUIET SITTING

THE SHIRK
UNWITTING EXORCISM
NETTING FIRE RESIDES
HANGING PULLING HAVING
NO CORRECTIONS CHANGE
LINES DIVIDING MOMENTUM
SUCTION TOWARDS THE OTHER

EMOTIONAL VACATION
IN THE MIDST OF A WORK
NIGHTS FORTY DAY BLOWING
FORTY NIGHTS A DANCING ELK

I LOOED BY HER STOP
THIS IS THE TIME ENCOUNTERED
INCLUDING MISTRAL DENOUNCEMENT
OF CREATIVE SKIN ENERGY

GROUND MOIST FOR APPRECIATION
ATTENTION DRAWN IN VARIED LENGTHS
LONGING CONTROLLED NOT LONGING
SOFT RESERVATION IN ONE BODEE

MOTTS COVE BLACKBERRY MASSAGE
MEMORRING STRICTIONS PURER IN

DAHLIA'S CHRYS AND THE MUMMY
STALE AIR IN BONDAGE
IN ADMIRRORANCE

DRAGON NO BREATHE
STUTTERING FIRE
JUMP OUT SING LOW FLY
CLEAR RISING TENDRILOFT

DRAGON NOSING
GUT CHOKE BUBBLE
SPRING OUT OF BRAMBLES
AND DIVE IT UP A NODE TICKLED
DRAM DRAM THE GLUING BIRD
LITTLE CAN SLEEP IN THE
LAUGHING TANGIBLE DISTANT
QUESTION CLEAR RING NO MORROW

"NEW YORK NEW YORK"
SAY IT TWICE FOR THE BITE
THE OBSERVER IN AN OPTIMUM
CLOSED VIEWING SHELTER
ON INERTIAL ISLAND MOVES
UPWARD AND AWAY FROM
UNKNOWN GRAVITATIONAL
DOWN AND OUT INTO ACCEPTED
MODES OF OBSERVATION

TWO DOGS FUSING FUR AND
WEEDS EXCRETING THE EXCESS
AS FIRE TO FLY OVER THE

CLEARFIELDSHINING UP THE GLOBE

LARGE EYES CAN MEAN
SMALL TALKING MYOPIA
IN THAT O TOO CAREFULLY
CLEANING OUT THE WEEDS THAT BIND

THE SELF SUFFICIENT MOTHER
OFF WITH THE KEYS TO THE WATER

"MARTIAN FOLK SONG":

SHIRLEY SHE KNOWS NOT
THE POWER OF BLINDNESS SEES
ALL THAT SHE CAN AND IS
SCARED BY THE REST
BEATRICE TRIES LEARNING SOME
MARTIAL LINGUISTICS GOES
ONLY SO FAR AS HER HOUSE
SAYS SHE WILL
BE——MORE——
STRONG THAN HER NEIGHBOR WHO
NONETHELESS WHISPERS
THE TRUTH IN ONE EAR
BE——MORE——
WRONG THAN HER NEIGHBOR
SHIRLEY AND BEATRICE
THE MOTHER OF THE DOGS

I TOOK BIG POSITION ON THE AMBLE

TRUCK LINGLING YELLOW I SMILE
I SMOKE RUMBLE SUCCESSIVE
CHAMBER BOWLS HOLLOW
(CHAIN THE EXTRA RING ON KEY)

OFFER BONES TO THE LONELY WRITER
IN TRUCK FLANKED THREE SHAMAN
TIGERS HE WANDERS A CROWD IN
TANGIERS WHAT WOULD LET THIRST
BLOWING DRY THE WAY HOME JAZZ
BEHIND CHINESE ROAD TO
TOMORROWS MAP SPINNING
MODERN PARTICLES FASTER
RINGS NEW AND COLORS
SOUND LINED UP AND HONKING
THE PARTED MUD LINES WAN MY
BRAIN THREADING THICK CLAY
CONNECTION TWIXT ERRANT FLOW
OBTRUDING THE COMMUNICATION
BELOW MAKING FA THA BLUE
DIZZY HAND STUCK TO THE
MIRROR CHATTER
BIG WORDS SOUND
BIG WORDS SOUND
BIG WORDS SOUND BIG

BLUEMOUTH TOO EASILY SECRETING
PUS RELATED FUZZ AS MOLDY NOISE
AS NOW RISES LOAMY OUT OF
CHORDBATH SINCERITY
TOWARDS AND UPWARD WEEDING

STOPS PRODUCE VARIOUS PITCHES

I MOAN AN OVERTONE
QUIVER ON LIPS OF HEYLA

GROWLING SYNTHESIZED DRONE
IN HARMONY WITH PURRING
EAR BUZZ OF FICTION
"WORDS, TIME FOR A CHORDBATH
OF PUNGENT APOLITICAL SOUND"

LIGHT AFTER STALKING STILL
AWAKE UNDER DREAM PILLOW
PROTECTING AN INDEFATIGABLE
EARTHFACE BODEE OF MOVEMENT
WATER TRICKLING SPRAYING
PLAY OF NOISEFED GRATIS

ONLY DISTINCTION
TWEAKS THE THEN KABBALAH NOW

ITS A GRAINY OCCUPATION
THIS SITTING A ROUND GULPING
REFLEXOLOGY OF GENDER
JOIN HER WITNESS THE
GRAYFACED SOLARITY
SONORITY IMPRESSION

I SAID HER THIS NOVEL
APPROACHING HERETIC CAUCUSES
BRAINVOID CALLUSES
GARAGE EARS

WHO FLOWS THE PEN BRA
PENUMBRA WALKING

A STATIONARY LEASE
ON AQUATICISM

musik: polyak
THUNDER IS SOUND IN CIRCLES
OR DRUM TAPPY DUET BARS

(JA JA TILL THE DUNE CAVES IN)

WHERE HOLDS THE NASCENT BEAN

PINKSHOT OUT OF
HER OWN VOCABULAR

CALMFIDENCE NESTING
CARDAMOM SWEET IN THE
OTHERWISE STANDING LOO EASE

NO SLEEP TO WAKE
THE NASCENT BEAN
FROM STOP TRAP SLUMBER

THE FREE SPEEDER
WON'T ARGUE A DISC
COMFORTABLE PASSENGER

MIRRORNUTS CRACK BETWEEN
OVERTHOUGHT ANGLERS
CRACK BUT NO OPENING
SO FRUITY NEXT PASSAGE

I NEVER LAY DOWN TO CATCH
BALD SPOT IN HAND UNDER

HEAD TWIXT THE DICTION
TRA LEELA LA TRA FAL ADOR
THE LACKLONG SURRENDER TO
THE BITTEN ACTION HOPPING
AND BLINKING RUN-ON WRITER
RUNNING ON A COOLER ON A
MORNING PORCH OR ROOF SIT
FUZZY BUDDHA NATURE NOINGS
A CLEAR POSSIBLE FIELDS
AND UNCLE ORCHARDS PITS
OF CALMING GREEN DODO
TAKE ON AND GO OFF BURN
EDGES WITH SPHERES OR
WITH CHILD ON SHOW SO
TELL BEATRICE AT LANDING
THE FERRY NO MORROW A
STEEL STRIPPED PAGE OR
THE CREAM OPPOSITION
O BLEARY INTELLIGENCE
SPEAK TO MY WOMAN MY
LEFT HAND NO MORROW
KNOWN NECESSARY FUNCTION
FOR SHARING THIS MOUTH BLUE
COMMUNIFORCATION PERHAPS
WILD ORCHARD WAS SEEDING HER
SLY BEHEADNESS WITH PRESCRIPTIVE
COMPASSION AND CONTROL
BEYOND A TENTATIVE TALKING

pinkshot
through the
unknown

family
roads
she said
trains
never leave
and making this way

josef juju
the morning
marimba man

pulsing partner
play on my travail
rain bowels and
beet jealous pandas

pinkshot
in the streets
of botswayla

leap ten gulps
of bayla tree
putona lap
comfer nut

pinkshot
outside the covet
of biography

landlines are the switch

on top of the juice brain
when feelings twale
—— the breeze

degrees and fields of

throb drone
about to be

mountain of tendency
muck rate choir
(nebula)

the ambidextrous patient
under the guise of an
ailing griot waggered
into her favorite station
daunting the known
necessary the erring
function gulped
a patient dosage
of lentements brewed
in oxygen grass
the first she'll reaffirmed

the doggone lassitude
came on a fudge
behind the crying
sag downstairs

she was swinging

bear dervishes
the next day

pinkshot

flat face green following
following soft time
up the route
delicious
tremendous
gaps
new fire
your face
open
finger tempting

want a manual shoot
jeeting knave mudman

words power a press
sore lean flack under
the vacant awning

skip in the extra tail
past offered set of
applied species——
zone out to nothing
demand of exception
ask faster the habit
of bean being bean

to type the running

writer guessing print
of farway gender

half longing
for nothing
demand of all
tones and scentenses

the forced to beyond with
the overwith jumping flat
viaduct first the diaction

sore circle reminded
of deep ice capped fashion

falling over the perfect edge
upon waking a dayskater
rings ka behind it

ka formal fantasy

pinkshot

the ambidextrous
patient dancing
pink circles a
cross the gridwell

webbed muscles
numb for the longing
be at all too cunning
and immediately prosperous

of a fast and sweaty complosion

quick over wonder
ing ing bear sways

musik craters
of another molecule
trust in the fingers
of modern dining

ONION LEAVES,
HER MAP UNTENDED

(1986)

(a love-tome at my wakemaster mad>sf>mad 6-21-85)

Fashion seat melts, so why heated? In standard garb of the infantile laboratory, she tones gonads french to treat her nascent franchise. Seated golden, quiver templars & pleated landings driven outlash. Was walking hindsight, a rare funky gennu. Instant normal rhythm. Freely-clawing jackal had harbored dancer. Harmonium earring. (Sleeping kicks her rising notorious; she's nurture worker stocked in wares over there.) Divorcee cracking jeweled jew a friar lifting the naughty ocean. Childhood screamer delve tonguing gymnastics in a treacher chamber. Her wings are redressing fingers: Yearner fraught with flailing. Mine or worker, seize the fairy. Very very all too va va skitting. (Drifter laden, "Made in Heavier.") Flymap sticks to her over shoulders, nipple thinking. The mime. "I'm rigor set in cloudless," to herself. No substance runs this tonic or I zulu trespass liver. (Hunger rivets on solider station.) "You spray my pore-walls, remind me I'm water." These girls play pansy while their men call. She riding her own beau underskin & pours only firmly. Feather skeptic balks. Chain gangs of feeling driven while operated. Minute trespassings delivered up death-path. (Rain cells her converted waves.) The click is on! Theo trails. Over-blown headmasted delays, "You're railing on," fetal disposition. She believe she believe. (Even polluted, girl reduced is enlarged.) Air pocket aware of itself only spaces between chords. Clouds are solid; direction is naught. Her majesty required haws & gains so races headward. Highroad falls asleep by the way, encounter craters & throws the boulder in. (Listen, the splinter blinks.) Wine couldn't make this jello sane at her lover, or even in. She jabs hotpoint with her distinction blurring communiqué. Gently billows he psychic skin as solid as color. The round-mouthed afraid of rooms, just stepped in a fairly groomed bereft. This solarcoasted squeaking a tune, "Isn't all play the train connection?" (Rings too subtle for years.) Figuring nothing. Mood of sandwiches torturing beetles. Races needle-proper sound popping repeat. so conservative of wasteful miser, diamonds riding alone aren't sparkle. Stuped. Go nuts on ahead. Something near: hurtle spray. "Just too large & sophisticated," turned green & didn't know it mammy. Tripper pushed to please you lowered her job for the use of it. Metal cleats or wildest swimmer on a cat claw for gratis. (Fuck-kneed faithful informer.) So that. The earth betrays ten surface facts. Follow a dozen. Internal logic barely combustible, metaphors tangle while attention strays. ("I only something never matter.") Fresh frozen harnesses, soaked & broiled, drag him again furled over. Make this writure an incantation. Ballooned not doomed, I sneeze it coming, hero. (Where so.) We seize the same two blue-red airwater. I tone; you gamble. You're my flight attending, check for the rest of my baggage. I push you in the water; you tag my undertoe. The foam crests beneath us a taste of sorbitol. Breakneck surrealist unhinged by flapping mounted gate. Ware. Wear. Wheres. (In the middle of unction, a trapeze whore.) Nails & skin unintended, a feline walkman shrouds the nearest clearing. She enters her loaded myth, touches it hung with glow & adjourns the crowd with her wielding. Artstick abundance is fervor shocked trying but strewn with a guess of self. Signs, to what. Oiseaux of undaunted beatitude steps out of her giggles & onto the sand. Asides flapping & fell off, her mind drilled a barrier. Bit somewhat stronger or foreign intruder. Ocean of happening welcomes Ophelia, & a tingle reach tests her dry-mouthed and yearning. Her eyelids battle weeds black. (Whether she hears herself humming in the next room.) Reminder diving the grandeur. We licked flypaste & hurdled sticky seats, nostalgia, graffiti & bubbles. "You wouldn't let me in last time." She never-members, "That must have the lair, Honey, without the rows stocked." He hushes. The queen turns a turtle: arrives quiet when I'm most awake, mania herself. (Softer skirts & many's a hun.) Check for it again, looking out windows, banging shingles. The gigolo yells, "Look at this." Lolling afterworn, halo reddened. The grasses greener possessing entrails. This afterwhich fluffens formaldehyde wetter, too badly conditional. Sucks friction at pointed, if not hotspur stracted, concocts denotions emoted last from reality. (A refrain does so joyously.) No lake drop in uniform shanties, but forever the moss bug of chivalry. Deliver, ask the goldman one-question sounds. Detonates exploring the next city. "You're the book I refer to no matter of deference." We fly over dry white river on right wing. Squeeze it lady stuck to screen with own breast of things "loving the ages." Lysenkoism. The men dance again free inside their motion. The ontology of a gene equals what matter. The china bell advertisement has flagrant lion on a jumping tin terrace. Liquid smile divinely the duo. Iron mind, "no wonder its" selfconsciousness triangle, machine people sustaining bellicose vane. Genuine generous flyer wrestling the anger above-face. Phalanx dirty in the napkin chef of favors: "Bewiggle my ordinary gushes." Froth iron giant cervix from early farmer yesses with tendrils extended. Ears only slowly, groin supertended, homely turning grounded without friendly. Boxing in common with a dizzy ship.

Shuffles wakeful quiet. Terrestrial excess bending steady unknowing dip into highrose. Shoes off bantering. The distance from fairies the farthings repented. Sure-shine or turned off. Machine-chest choked hegemony arrived at. Plain organization for the other man's habit, I disarray porch or pansy throb overreach. Mismarking et al. the hug mirror wrinkles enlargement. Forensic temple, this umpire's nonetheless mystery reduced to suspense. (Her connoisseur promises hushtones for the three in the picture seated opposite.) Feel in the blank unaware. Of the juices all chocolate calms. Psychology fingers endure. Loudspeaker of certainty, no wait an answer. The sorry game endangered ease. Piano in the corner somewhere engaging. "Oh isn't that why because." Walk this way in some circles a hundred minutes later the same thing.Creaky axle seers concentration unless saturated. Bewitch, the chatter: bloodleaf in company. Overgroan excitement otherwise distracted by an earful of sex-thrashy music fucks the unearthly maiden. Up out of & in touch. Talk to break between sentence, to bathe before noontide, she hesitates stately the ideas like pajamas. Pollution worries this granite-nut tender. Laughter is homogenous reliance out the back door in a flashy pants. (Type justifies the wandering.) the explorer stumbles over trailmarks, cursing the numbers irate nonstop cuticle. A breath before penning, vibrant inner-aural prowl minus the sun or a new distraction. Unrecorded volume the atlas of her going. Silent. A modal detail hollowed to nothings diminutive. As if stuck on a gleestring, self standing above, her hands hit headshine: too far, only the globe. I haven't rainier atom for current brave wanes. "Got the pin holes filled? Shift the borders up, tighten out the trinkets, & belie those goads homeward!" In the gravy, wrinkle. Swat. (Attitude adjusters are pounding percentage while the bare girl treads lace.) Bargain equals feathers. The circle people pry the rings closed which gashes erased by similar pie. Wording the moths of other tables. "Got a knowhow to twist 'em just right." The subtle makers of a terror master might fragrance the captain: This is the carpet my landmark destroyed. Long sentences, spindly words strung on a railroad, delay. Forest walker forced to hitchhike, to no one course is the diver relegated. Uniformly the treadmill freezes. Comfort called for later removal. Sharpened proverbial pencils, the drill master forgets his homerun. "Who left the door open?" (Assertus withdrawn.) Busy humming cilia turn wet on a mental hot, letting chaos reside. Juggler fangling new direction with cistern over-growing perk. La-va-la, la-va-la. Lydia a buzz on the outskirt. Forked receiver, she tampons majestic higherings. Violet's yearning found artery in books. Taken, the fact that a dog seemed nylon. Leveller of intoned fantasy, he's calm with a breath of salt. Ice jeweller glitters, her benign complexion traveling secretions. Fellatio harnesses a wicker saddled cinescopic. "Try my deliver." (The love people are saturated with fantation.) Obelisk miracles sprout & rebound. Her heart-drench faked the sun into umbrella they pulled lung. My dictionary, this man who sings. Own international paradise glowing, she's tricked into enormous rhythm. Brotherliness & of the soeur, those pocket words are for middling. Madbathhousewarmers cuddle his or her verdant but mythical files. Cats lipping sounds like wind. Own relaxed relations grew in the neighboring pod. "For years," makes the mod—both sweet, pie & apple. Seventh major retreat: feel firm fingers again. This rare another body man. Needful delusion shared a navel. "Won't look-at" man isotropic. Climber inspected darker sounds than "J." (The earlier movement light & affected.) Lung blue & clean water cat-happy but dogent. Riddled caffeine body watching lookers familiar. Anonymous entry sustained hesitation with delightful equestrian itches. Turbo monday. Luscious window travel dubbing still oddly different hues. Grab the terrarium pane so ashtray can blend with nesting. Eyestorm keeps treading the farmland laden with carytas. She burns stages aside the tall harmonium, unclassic meeting under the harbor. Awares qua non. Faces shelter the strange aquarium. Long run in a cherry bout. Cul de sacking orange bedlam with a clammy contraption. Surrender. Miso only, groining trappist towards flood-level noses. Lion aroused blue dog tracks into unprecedented drive: she's harmonizing fly wings & train biters. Formula H.T.O.R. (Hetero-clawless fieldings?) Omniscient slicker engages in fanfare. Zilch. Twang. Undone. When the "Duty Boss Literal" saloons into lunge position, antennae wilt. The weather-watcher is undeterred. She gruffly rebirths tossing worms, even tramples radiance. (Umbrella popped, listing lists of dozing.) Homo-culpability. Circle-tips imbibe. Variegous with heart-felt incandescence. Or, rabbits die lonely. Given sharing, ice could melting. A priori mister is yearning throughout this buttocks, tending swelling before tension. Gushes would enthrall the commissioner of anti-tragedy, but short throaty hiss incurs. Re-again gin. Hourly fructose. Meandering. Boy wears talisman with pigment relief. The woman nearly lost her camera in brave hot touch with sutra-diviner. Onion is an ordinary seasonal cookie, a wakeful lemur who usurps a tandem. (Rigor mortis indicts the lake long survival feature.) Bargain behind, the trail bender bows to worn gravel. (Plain miracle once dormant.) The every which way settles for eggs.

One taste-specific passenger in an outboard arrangement: side by die, north by delivery, fearing distended. King vested tranquil channels in conspiracy. Swimmingly fucking her bewilderer outpoured. Zig position sagging, that tendril wrinkled, nosedived. “I’m underways, water-dog.” Pressures balanced, this tipsy inherent porn circle relished the data & enobled the tomes. Rhyme adjusts her hem. Submission for frequent vantage. Creeper obelisk, once again baby ocean. Trees pissed on daily mirror a matrix. Arrival was extended, as is.

onanism curdles

(1985)

cash reins.
smooth tail

hideaway.
fluv,
dairy sound.

the tell remain.

jiggle lap.
the prairie.

mannered acreings,

cellbinds flicker,
deeper rigor
wraw an undermined.

the log that quays
rejoinder.

wha phail.

ploog tid humilier.

grain tinkles.
water lingers.

dry. huge. foaming. air.

tomorrow eye capulet.
expectator jewels
aforementioned alight

tradewind.

sucked outward galog.
princess swat
flavoring rancher.

bog mason numbered.

dramoular casoons,
lens held carotine
surfer, overauto.
inner water.
intraseculum.

trough brand.
lard ways.
zillion hybrid normal
cracker obelisk.
hydro pawn.

digits sanction,
lestera mauber.

frame. turn.
coffee. bhagwan.
cecil. book. key.
mustache. sandal.

hardware.
lover awning.
retardage.

scolding
chased awake.

ferming pasto,
weed puréed.

jonny retains caste
recall oilier flymap
steel circular amongst.

horrarium.
senegal.
troinard.
heth al atum,

rearing.
sarchof.
gripp.
hedondulate larving.
said tobaccum.

unit honorary
quilted feron.

herald removal.

nonquist clothing herapit.

grapes,
may,
dancing,
crumble,
reheat,
dowsing,
transpire.

request erring.
soakage revile.
nostril deflecting.
ruminette.
dump.

surprise lasting
elbow sufficient archwave.

speaking.
stalking,
drown leveler
constation agog.

it.
between.
those. caesar.
cast. trot.

trampling.
icestorm.
inhale.
sister.

avalanche teeming,
nightfall adjusted,
maxims hush orange,
woodbox recover
pliable tone,
fascinate,
evolves,
inhabit selfhorn.

re structure.
manic prepare.
bewilder looker.

push cleaver,
rebibe.
emulate th.

smother rewind
membered bother
surfeit charred longer,

waste impales
own usury.

hector during,
imply potion,
register differents.

felon stalls home, cocked.
postkettle urgent.
needleless summit.

avoid.
derange.
infigure.
zohast.

glue-rate compost.
hatch invalidate.

ingestible,
enlarge
occasion,
taboo bedlam.

perched. entrap.
zygote allotted.
sheffeliere. hum.

enreach
opulent
hermitage,
monterey.

zephyr
abling,
croach,
fragment.

kale
mediate.
urban zither.

sidestep arrangement.
spectate orwell
answer. shocks.

deliver undress.
remake upper,
zoned dehors-zone.

catalogue freer,
overgrown dusk game
witch walls.
viscera?

cling objective
filth.
shed.
rusted.
cool.
enfinger.

shraft tilted.
belittle flank.
exhume.

entable headmouth.

dented, singe,
kaleidoscope,
forestry, turquoise.
elaborate vial.

rigby.
reasoned
kerchief.
hallow
potash,
piranha.

harlequin.
chillum.
climatas.
germridden.

every lines other

(1985-1995)

Continuous piece on tape. Cut with various textures (self doing this: "Look I'm"). Look blankly at mountains. Stop, move. (Multi-phonic held buzzing, radio static, shortwave song.) Loving this woman again. The same one tone. He shuts the radio at lean three in out loud new tongue book on words dressing. My hand backseat the pencil will type on later. The self sensing of a book from love looks up in a bridge, under the Mississippi. The reader forgets which store she's in, "lost in" or "NAIL BREAD." Signs are everywhere. Niches imagined. Four fire hydrants stacked, yellow/green, red/orange on top. (A glance extended to renovated permits; our house before my self. The voice hearing itself. Slows down. Car hum recedes. An all at once delivery excepted, "Where cows are boars & books are people." (Gravel clicks. The logs of the house she grew up in a year were brown fences & brown garage. She singing with engine up the other wise, remembers the view.
Sugarloaf is rather creamy then brown turned yellow & purple in spots for late October. I asked it where Ann Sykes lives & it finally spelled AZ. Goodbye. Louis Zukofsky. I am his wife & I know I have turned in this direction. "This is Coon Valley!" he mimics his explanation

I retrieve my pencil thoughts.

We begin
to be able
to see
the page
as shapes
set in

cross offs
stand out. "Blanks create no alternative."

Robert calls his brother "void head" but his mother refuses to talk about matters of the mind. (Who IS the voice that here is a sentence that sings, & that eye is no organ in clusters parading, out of time, POLYMETER, capitals blacker in some, stances or stanzas in groups of others. Creak the door open: simple words mince cheese. Another town taken, "kwiktrip," cramped inspiration.

At home with the toaster & the telling, cat & child fed each other well. Two hands exchange a key which later stroke backs in embrace. Ah, K or C, we're joint witnesses on this burly boat, does there ever shake a ladder over board? That night, three admire (smirk) a barred woman whose huff pardoned the waves. (That one again never tucks powder up tooth out of satchel.)

This stop will be nightly. A ways from the sticking edge, long after music: the grind smells delightful. Circles arriving full circle dance up the aisle with eves. ChooChoo remembers the word for neck. Let off to each other, I say of my back. Not simply switched, but broaching the meaning. One continuous right past the place to stop where the neck releases dream-words.

Self at causes. Talkers "over there" for anew looks familiar. Rather "on that side" or "incommunion," i sit in MY "art world," we who sit on our ceiling. Words impart or words impasse or are they used as heard. They tick-idio agreeing; pompous ask me what i do. For the water-poor fed ones i paid forgetting first forever push.
"Ten thousand grunts & no solutions!" The chalk line strays. Budged: a heavy word stirs, blinks. Adaption.

Destruction: I bear my answers & they are obvious. "Obviously" I am oblivious. Told across the ocean, I swim in for reply: I swim alone. The aloneness of a mind that's the middle of much, with holes or walls. Loving too, we're side of two stumps, no trudgery but unaware shackled. I swim foreplay: erotic distraction or dissected line. Another door.

Music back ground. Each majestic highering good, this beauty under pulling grip out. Going into binary, this & this, boulder stepped on, I'm hoping their conservation is still music. Anticipating conversational comfort. Ragged reads punk. Interval of generation? Rush hands into water before unlocking the bike with the moon gleaming. Darn joy. A darker man re-enters. Even dashed. The seriousness of love crawls in further. Do you hear the laps & layers over the background? I keep wishing I were thralling.

Divorced from all coming, fried past the sound of sizzling, aside my arm pages of letters. The clock has the same face, but this morning I was dreaming about swimming & cake. Re past friend now female "stitched before graduated," grateful I had to do with it. The mind oils rubber to turn around to see it. "It doesn't & it does" as a sentence mimics a genre. Not to be tempted. Or aware of itself, isn't that game? Winners don't think. As the one-studying-the-book's outside next to me. "Dangling" is a word describing an achronology of words: Is as enclitically removed? Surgery rhymes with a lie. Cause I saw it through to the other side of the tracks. Near exclamatory over the access to a personal metaphor. "My own" "but how can the writer presume." In other worlds, your train or mine. That one might claim a signifier, strung or single. Metaphors as assets, or even words that stand for books. "Higgling" for example is not even the title, & yet I see its cover with that stacked name amidst colors & others hearing it. A word means tired, so someone offers a drug. How long was the session? (Play might arrive at any moment.) The parentheses remind her of onion leaves, but only a few might guess. Presumption is rather sure thrill with an inkling for sharing, aside from actually flapping arms with that reader. The closest leaves share a look of face, however, in view of the words which were last written.

Turning every word to leaf lies in color with a rhyming of head.
An aligning past the point of flight.
Words asleep fell to the ground with no order under the same tree.
Gathered, I at least scatter behind myself.
Who kicks the mud is the question.
I know this is a honing, some sort of growth or pre-growth, as if the bud weren't a leaf.

Distraction, the smother of perception. Upper arms stand for one volume erroneously titled "Love"; the one-way signs every which way lining the direction of the thought itself is another, no problem but something to be changed. Even but makes for contention. Better the rear end, we smile. And perception plunges below the conversation level, "How can woman know injustice & do injustice" still no one asks the question. I recognize the modems of division, but I haven't tasted of the root enough to fortify its leaves. Thus I remain in pile. "Too many people being nowhere at once," he snarls in synchrony.

Ruling out the lone hill or for now, the base of that thinking tree, I watch the centered one not consciously selective, nor conscience of condition, one arm under the dishes, cleanly arranging lines of thought. I press my feeling into you, make a lasting, VOCA LIES. How many trains go by before I look up? Even as I write. No right to be called odd, or often ordinarily asleep. Or pert at the wrong station. The greeks make noise to say "meaningful" long & drawn out. Forward remembers something new.

Slipping on the colors. The raw arm of the pencil, or the flood of paint tamed: xexoxial warlings, hearing the font limey seismic contusions. The T spills over into kaos.

Subliminal roars; this spelled right, that combusted.
Catching hold of. And also sound, which reminds us
of snow: quieter noise. And this strange quiet woman
stepping read her writing, shy & articulate, a close
opposite to me.
Even encounter. Each perception. Dreams ailing food
across stomach, intimacy that would otherwise come
unhinged, remembered. I am every owman, hearts there,
more is here. Unconnected signs. Or sighs beginning
a whole thought. Never ending? Equals sameness, or
duration, which changes.
Figuring it out, when otherwise stuck in a circular
emotion. Such thought detaches itself, a start.

Red seethrough light bulb on its side, vibrating like a cricket. With eyes closed, I see my body standing triangular: pregnant in Bisbee. Silhouette of wooden buildings at morning. The words are too heavy & I drop them. Do they tell a story or is there none? "I'll take Melissa." But the characters aren't met, except under the heel. Somebody's been in every town, for years. Touch that clearing of the more around my aural.

The "born writer" "has it." This hazard is over, the ear next to meaning. At a turtle's pace or in a turtle's place: the ink boils in my cauldron spilling on the lines. But not matching the thickness of thought, the nap gets creased. Like waking up before going asleep; fabric of mind uncertain. (My narrator wants to sit in the station again & wait.) All the while, apparent looking on a nest of feelings, a net selfstrong, the deftness glaring when no conflagration.

Forward in a ring.
Glands for marriage.
Hot belief churns the blood downward, you're all the man.
These commas are like lines, lay them out, one after a spell, the

next match burns hotter.

> Always the flair, ended with a certainty, nor brass, nor chair, not gumbo. You affair staged spontaneously trespassing lest rhyme be the heart. Beat the joining, man fortress. Still this listing, poised, shifts hearer tempest. In turn all the sun.

M isn't bothered, not another thought, on to the next thing.
L recounts the mishap, weighing gold or dirt.
I did feel at home, taking the freedom to grunt, stretch, or borrow.
I'm more toward than they know.
A splinter crack in my muddied crystal "no room no room but do come in."
Is an unending radio in the space below.
I can picture you drawing your space in that house with invisible strokes.
I can see you better now than when the ants had their blindfolds on, inviting me to watch them. Talk.
A criminal in the company of proud new laws, taken aside to talk of deviation, "You're one of us as I tell you this & yet we assume you know nothing."
On the contrary too much unsettles my present standing here, waiting for the suspension to break as if one of them might wake up, who dares to dream of his own power. "Or her." I am a monger eating the wrong words.

In the advantage of time cleanly love "minus the" where I can see how easy it is to be red. Eventuring the moistest dark cold corner grows a greenish glow that looks at you & is deeper. Dreams again a mentor, one like a rabbi teaching winds & one a woman you have to enter a floor way above a climbing you whine but have made it before. Fear & relief, forbidding with love. As I bleed, a blur is dissolving. The stuff cages are made of is forged by the same jaw: strong & pouting. (Semantics are an association wet in the dressing room but here "out of line.")

I wasn't the stops or the spots or the way she connected them but the fact that they skipped over something or something was was repeated. And over and the same line, missing an other curve of things. Even now gaily resentencing an old hog.

Feeling good equals not the desired state, nor does looseness always open the lover's equilibrium. Mine heart quivers thoughts of a woman who lied & marred us both in her retraction. No word each day equalling former days called consistently mornings now no mourning enables movement. I salve the jagged holes left swollen & tender, though we need whole remedies for renewal.
And my wings house another, alone on his own who yearns too much my curving dominance. So I lie as well, I do & I don't & sometimes I breed further addition which my first deems subtraction (from distraction). Mine whines at outer edges, free from heart strain thus unsafe for flying. "I thank you for difficulty," though sincerity had only just met.

Allowed to play with crumbs late at night, I tear the license in half, as it was not given.

The very mirroring of time as I walk up this street, squinting to not see in order to mirror myself ahead. "Lodged again in the place that doesn't happen," the glass blower reflects flatly. Whether the boxer falls asleep in the ring or my tongue instructs a thousand men to wield, I forget.
It is then I get to close up & go home, when few have gone & I am left alone to bother.

Living by the clock of a generic diary while theory lies in disarray. Why it's tempting to borrow from science, you even wonder about dream synapses evenly escaping from time. (A perfect simplicity stood there again & again for re-view.) Perfect as a prefix.

"Wakests" is a word complied in a row of wooden letters, large & salmon like the body, which moans to speak for itself.

Having spoken, at least a clean page forward, my body forgets all but the taste of mint. Only when you hold the numbers up to it does the losing equal the loss. Something's got the turnover. The orgasm expends & declined to let go.
A winter oscillator, list these things for attention, this rack & that line, curved up around the mouth. All holes holding hands, meaning the bodily exchange if universal is more than body.

Wakeful concern over the time being. This itch shadows that pain. That I can feel to its bottom, mixed-up with love. Sadness can happen as well. Welled up, but not walled within. Listening for some singing, the shutting door would do. No blood on the snow, invisible ache times to confound.

Beside me an age-old youth. I shared his loincloth & his cell dream. This man has been there & back while I was learning to play it. He was my sister before I kissed him is how I know. A bicycle tire doesn't always turn into a night upstairs, sometimes the sleeplessness carouses a memory.

Stuck on the couple with the gray pants & cane.
The piece of paper without the cookie said, "When we have not what we like, we must like what we have."
Compassion & love on two sides of the snowbound street.
Everything fits, even the bites & the woman yelling at her dog.
And the thing keeps turning.
I am not owned again I forget my heart spun straight head.
As in orthos, for of course this is not ordinary.
She looked at me, behind us.
She knows no drama, she lives bizarrely as naturally as I play an accompaniment.
(Wondering if cold *is* seeping in.)
Doubt is a fungus we rub into each other.
You salve quietly: I hug into it.
See, this budding is for you.

But bugged by any number of incestuous habits of removal, you dig us gravely misunderstood.

We let our eyeballs leak at our leisure, the way the tomkins do. One movement cracks the bell, which like leaves vane in fractured direction. "My heart in a paper bag," the thinker knows. (*She* had invented an urgency.) He singing the song I dropped. "Paper bag full of Waaaater." What reverberates is farther south. The reflection of which I am. With a hat & another, two tongues as ill. Tripped again over herself too quickly. Words rumble by as usually they traverse, occluding heart thought & language as well.

I could have cut out the crackling, precluded the scar, initiated a strength.
Which pace grows change all the deeper more gentle.

A duo-persona has its own unhyphenated identity, one said "quoi de faire," live quotient of bean. That two things can exist together at the same time as one lights the candles on the table. M & N, in sequence a pair; M & W, on top of each other; M & A, a way to communicate; L & W, on either side of "A." Without the itch, a family can't communion.

A firing of lines welcomes witches in. Opening teeming stuffed. The gale breaks on a mind of its own, while yonder drifts, the snores rhyme & hedges tilt. "Squirrels living in chestnut-shaped houses?" The "N" "in the family name," importance a mask in the mirror, looking for she who looks. Straight ahead makes one direction all the way around a map of psychology torn to shreds at our feet. Each piece rises in defiance of itself, asserting assertion, backed by blindness, lined up for the couch.

Grey.

From an empty white bucket I pick moist dust clumps.
I handle my breasts from behind.

Which hair approaches?
A velvet young boy.
Am I said, among the path, to be its ginger-edged witch?
Always tangy.
You forget how small bubbles can be.
The ground dies when too solid, disperses when drenched.
A plane to walk on, a pocketful of berries.

She would spread it all over the mouth if it were redder.
Born without a tub or hung on the doornail, only one of the remaining children actually built things from scratch.
Our knowing lies behind us breathing in no impatient manner.
Time, to leave.
Could be under suspension, taken over, pinched perfectly.
(Encasing air, encasing water)
"I remember now" means I built a floodgate.
Two must wakest.

Madly reconstructing language against a habitual harangue or passing off. Holding a policy, out to turn over feeling, let alone magic might vibration. "He's our," & not one of them, dares. Fears what they "we're a group I can't" and none does. No outlet means no opening, I'd be "outnow" too.

How to breathe with a pen: When the mind requires notation, the body must sit still. It is this kind of thinking requirement, here to catch them before they grow, these stray clouds of association with or without heart. Take care that the mind breathes first freshly.

I learn history & recall the smell of the future by juxtaposing two men. The second can be several, but only the first brews so darkly. Most life is he fungus-putrid-new-you-can't-ignore compared to we-circle-smilers-laugh-&-recall-the-same-cat. Growth itself smells funny. Ugly & bubbling. But am I standing still even air I write.

No way out when the two doors face each other.

I think that I am leaving myself a body of language. So that, reading their book, by then soiled like a bible & hopefully torn in places, we will remember things like the humidity of the polyglot's nature & the earliest time I excelled in parenthetical paraphernalia. However, it occurs to me that a body houses. Moved into & grow out of. Are metaphors more than gravy? Aimlessness at its finest——or lines self-deceived? I beware that these words, as written or as read, *satisfy*. Not unlike the tone of a saxophone when there is alas no song being sung.

"Mine." How deep grooves the possession. Infused & emblooded? Treacherous thin goes my reach for this one, while thick & embodied with all those seeming. And more to incorporate. The road is blind by this point. Holy magnified thought stuck staring at a single tree.

My Me-Kell: A sunken verdant road flanked by red. His younger face was just where over my sweet pug no age descends. How green can cold be?

ii. RE: TURN

Always an other.

(When the metaphor recognizes itself as a mask, or regarding the trip's rebound.)

Like that, why interrupt the smaller lines' preoccupation?

Rumbling up again after all these, you expect me to be moving before the door was open. Is it up *now*? And yet the garage always needed cleaning & I clearing & as I write the masks lift itself up higher in the seat & doors start flagging.

I waved neither goodbye nor hello this time: I can see without my eyes in both directions without turning my head. Sometimes the idea of history gets in the way, more often memory, but this line it was different. You can see it too soon enough that I am *writing myself smarter.*

Than play stills plays in this of mind marbled in experience. A return marks a return

I recalled Ida, who "recalled bathing," as we coin each other's lives.

Live fish at the china market are really dead but dead fish have lost their shine, their wet charm, I myself a stealthy one wily denying the relevance of an overseas expiration. In other words I wouldn't use the play of "Blare," rather his death must have been the private sound of an ache. I "got some out" describing him to an other, such a selfish language *he* escaped, though not "luckily."

I would've strangled him not to doom himself still he twinkles & horns in fact I many have read him dead wrong: that one who for period chuckled & awed might never have chosen the end.

That "no photos allowed" of the squirming seafood were allowed but then that shooting the dead was okay. I wondered & I still wonder. And that fish live in the duckpond.

In a child's mind the whole word is an object & a world; we say, "No, that's two words, an el-em-en-o pea."

Home equals new children, memories of being one, where I go back & where I return, where the key "you hold on to it" lets us in, how when you take the ess off, the power of the particular is lost but the cat is still confused.

Was he wondering to kill himself or was he perfectly sure? I'm not sure the depth isn't clouded by play nor that seriousness is required at all funerals. Some dogs like to roll in dead fish while their owners prepare them meat.

Coldness should at least chill me, rather I bristle hotly at a shoulder turned, hunched, or straight up its path. I don't know enough cold women.

Why death & love & such kinds lure content's dream onto paper, demand the attention of words. "I intend to exhaust the subject," she said of the manner in epic & gladly noticed a growth of dyslexia. How drinking tea with a writer can start a fire on paper a week later. Had the writer been a woman. Certain figures of speech are everywhere & in any position. As soon as you wear one for a while the fashion wears out of it. Is language itself the only other thing?

It's true the distraction of the distracted recoils from singlemindedness. Which large word can be a good or a bad thing depends how far out you want to lift it. I took the twinkle in my hot & wandering eye & squeezed the guts out of it as sorely a turtle run over. It was staring at alphabet colored paints dripping weird incredible music heard between his sleep, how gray can be yellowish out a nyc window at five in the morning perfect height above the streets, calmly lying in place even with the likelihood of rodents passing, I suddenly understood my pain. Which meant feeling it really. The Other, crouching hopeful, full-eyed. And the Other, crouching longing obedient.

This is not allowed, this cross-out of remembering better which image feels the text like a teenager. Where is the point. In taking a word for blatant. Sex has imposed more attention than death. Which hurts more. It was the train hit me, everywhere between my cunt & my heart & later on including each. As if I needed another excuse. I did, & it didn't work because when you excuse yourself you are no longer at the table but are someone else's meal. I admit I said "eat me." Still do, though I no longer use words or situations, the fantasy can be so quiet now I don't hear the moaning. (At least I threw up in the cleaner apartment.)

Matched with that place of the air of a top of my head. Or thinking with my eyes closed, a beard can make a difference. Looking at the wayside, I don't remember falling except for the response at having stunned someone. Pray he don't lust too long.

A way to think
A dead one
This big one will decide itself.
The blind never searing.
Seduced by the pair notion.
Warmth among the blind.
Green sticky liquid or a snuck glass of water.

Sometimes the march splits its rows.

"Let's see one you up." Really heard. Quotation marks could mean more than voice. The "only" of "you" ancient & still quaking. The browngold on the deadman's knuckles. Tickled by your inclination to awkwardly preposition.

Love can see deeply unconnected.

Self conscious without eyes?

Glue of prepositions & plusses is rarely influenced by others. I was my young pride in grammar & knew how to quote appropriate.

Brave unables. Do I display my thinking? Nessay. Green is hard to see, in ink.

Self-deprogram: To cut out the hesitation before the strike & not to remember the notches. Not to not forget but to be there before the mirror. Fie! We're vying *together*, I, lost on the wideness of range, I'm frozen inculcate. Paneros routinely in the closet, butane pre-measured. "Shut up" to myself separated again by small words.

When the respective in different perspective caught, a terrarium evaporates. Because of insomnia because of sleeping over because on aware. Yet the period bloats, stops *after* the dollar, leaves a piss of trail. It can be difficult to swallow, I'm still trailing the hindsight, see?

Leaving off esses, is this a stigma unimagined, a margin amassed. Only to be followed by references did it make sense. If my words were blind, look how the words look like it or look at it more closely described "forced madness." Until food got in the way.

You gotta admit Christmas.
What if you can't find a pen?
Do writers at night forget park benches.
I was almost asleep.
I fell into using past tense.
I often come out of it.
It flows like spaghetti.
The reversal is silly.
Sauce can be contagious.
If I ignore the lines, the table gets in the way.
Retyping hurts the back.
The sentence or the paragraph.
I resee writing.
A transition like the next day fresh.
Where we put the word "just," & the voracity of the thrust.
Put on top of the table.
A surface unintended & later detached.
An obsession with the future.
"With as against," propositions again winning.
I tried not to fight it, it would would occur.
Crumble the chunk or chew off a piece.
Had I forgotten the question?

Questioning answers is not equal to its obverse, which offers less suspicion.
The subtle relationship between S & C.
Is the new necessarily choppy?
Is all speech imitative.
After what follows who.
Delightful?
Is the difference without the question mark.
Are our minds really so similar.

An astrological sign which always asks, doubts.
Or is its relationship to the comment.
A C to the comma as an envelope to enclosure, cupped or capped.
Why is fascination so often mere?
Because I didn't spend eight months thinking about it.
How come she always knows when it's over.
I'll come tomorrow.
"Over tea," because I was too hung for the other.
Don't say "over" again.
Then quotation's elbows leave marks on the table.
I'm smarter than that.

Forced to, but already not flailing. Quickchange shifts old gear aside & scrambles up the icicle turned red. For a fusion of impossibilists, kipper frosting by the granule, shove consequence out of vapor.

Except with writing in the snow, the self-conscious kipper. To write music, to muse trials thru the deluge. Removed, to remotely misuse is to fracture ultimatum. Incessantly S-poor, gigantic. Fire away.

Misnomer: the side adjacent to the side. Delirium trembles? Not jack dismembered. (There's a certain modifying the amazement, if the gin soaked verses the icicles dried. Why this P again? In another modality, more recycles & drooling transfictions experimenting with dolls.) Do dictate my yearnings. Farthywell, honey stoned, gyrate solidly aglow might reflex music, & itches first mahab to be night.

Harken just, at this point, salamander garage dream reckons jist. Rations for rational fools. Political harangue, tigers extraneous, unforgotten bells ad, minus checkers or dummies which grin. Jesus saluted the heat going on, the oven crackling, the fire grapes toasted. Investure didn't know or care for easter much easier. Would've ricocheted, the refrigerator song took off. Like riveting feathers or stroking film of cock. Certainly not afraid to beat women, I take acception to my language, which is the way I cook words. "Cocky bitch" froths under cover. Opens her lids on pen "du pappiler". Even butterflies are hardassed, female. But butt butt. Deaf mutes are often men. All but disco. (And save your graces.) Pursestrings unlined.

Get out of it!
Periods detain
Lionness in rune
Drip
Clinch
Erectile
Nugget,
A more erotic word is slurp——
when embarrassment doesn't slug it
more than commas or capital lawns
depends where your located
arrows as fingers
icicles tented, why I?

Only years later, horny still upty scaredy nothing, motion of cats nearby sound of walking in the ears. Yet trapped in redhotness, too jumbled the screw falls tasted of trust. Of loam some of us asked it actually featured the speed of the pick-up. Too what? Kiss me again. I couldn't tell you if I tried.

The ocean upset it, a breach of dearth, another romance on the quarter, like twigs I exerted them but each dot corrupts me. "He" stands for himself, or how ever many mirrors. When he looks out & stays out maybe we'll sprout a vortex with child. "Gotta give". Self-conscious masturbator can't enjoy.

Train fades away before the thought starts running. Sparks over snores, comfy potatoes for writing. On one of those days where the splitting of ends leans up against walls, pink strip or retaining seething projectable. Poly among friends? But lost contact is forbidden, hatchings are closed, deep love is controversial. Shouldn't, but he shuts out sharing. And him & her. Never the perpetuation of a getting there, a looking for & finding, less a reaching & holding, of an other.

Jazzed on contact, she's lizzed in like company: anything but the follow through. Was it always this way? Or back to sawmill venues never had? Tired with a concentric head, of retaining maintaining detaining returns to places untrespassed by we's barely touching.

Possibly naked, the softness of thoughts together, for others, let alone laughtering. An out that's warm inside & not without leash. No gone for a walk left note, bound tighter than that: "Make me tighter". Confused lashings belittle me.

Polygamy has nothing to do with sex; a declaration of friendship pursued in the unreality outside time.

While marriage reads the mail together over the heat, how far can it share itself with a bad leg? (Hookers green is rarely worn by prostitutes.) Which sways which wall? The question becomes seasonal even before the door opens crosseyed with simulation & oftwhile neglected.

Black frenzy.

The word "environment" polluted by the word "fascist".

"Such vibrancy" sour as petty gossip, she pretends to breathe porcelain but inhales soot.

Helping others dig their own by assuming they will, grave assumptions are so gingerly passed. Red dripping on umber flesh: unavoidably extant. But blodn't oblit "live" spelled backwards.

Harm. "Think nothing of it."

Informant. "You know the type."

"The thing I forget with": memory, blank with action, stored on a calling card, who carries baggage so colorfully sloppy. Turns over in her.

A gigantic lift up to see better hurts not nearly in exchange the black man finally surrender the point & "see you" turns real.

(Wiggle notion spits self-continuous interraglio first kindled by her flaming.)

See how the saying goes after the candy's been taken. Smooth as silk. Theatrical hyperion= goddess gone black.

Dichotomous men-saints are beasts are beasts, oh bet me which acerbation tastes sweeter. Geography gotten in the way of the stars regrouping tongues in tastebuds. Is the voice catching low like elf frequencies? This makes tallness soft & hard. "Je suis audeur," the handmotioned doctor of fugue-thrust. " 'The earth smelled like mainly Russia: Zut, we did & we do. *You* dot me up or dagger bent off again in frequent delay even mourning 'after that, I knew I could...'" Not intended to be fulfilled, the bleach with the black out makes me the twelfth one harder to reach.

A heritage if turkey strut grounds the icekeeper a week in Padded Bloom on a terrestrial diet shaved of brand seduction whenever the mend feels right.

How long has it been since I've written & how did I know to come back at this point? Does the reader ever see the silences; while the writer lives, the reader simply turns the page.

Time has come. The dark waters are soft & still strong weeks lead a stone path through the brushes with bends in hands & glinting heart muscle. Unreality wins the hand against no metaphor stained straying. The man begs eccentricity.

Truly self-learned selves sleep stuck between retaining & the dry: One wall holds on while the other just won't melt. "Which bed are we discussing?" Confusion clears its throat, so don't doggerty trope saliva. Faith *in*: Speaking of bodies.

I'm like for welts come in two forms, from dyslexic throughout the binary gap to duplicity clouding over. Will she remember that word, any word, ex years from now? Probably not, nor do the nuptials rhyme. Thingamajig. This absurdity is an extra, it was found on the left side of the dining room do you care for water let alone the drinking of pleasure? (Warmed up again, "Quaking in my boots" will outtempt me in my Sunday shoes.) Is the pen any substitute? "The full moon has an erection, a sculpted face with its name changed downstairs." "It speaks to me" in swallowlike foreign tongue.

"'Swedish meatballs & that front door's open.'"

If it's not one thing.

The surface of memory is nondescript compared to the event itself. The days previous had sizzled, a suggestion to others to spring. Glee & fear rode shotgun together until the latch was pulled. I was "her" & she toyed with my name like a familiar tongue as we noticed the world was over. Seven forms between we who were disintegrating thus reunited. Old dogs tricked into revival after the fact which maintenant lies subliminal.

Every aftermath a new stage: the seafarer couldn't drink enough while the captain licked yet another edge. The two mighties looked alike from the new height, a fact the glass eye superimposed sans the aid of sight.

1988-89

THIRD ENTERING

(every lines other pt III)

In a world without lines indeed circles would hang on. Four in the mornings cheek soft for whimpers, squeak grunts & back cries into calm sleep & tit-filled smirk. Over earthen fire but wet, regularly while fed nightly. "My——" with no sense of possession rather to give over & up times.

The throb into a future fusses plentifully. Guarded, we ward off habit & sing gardens, not to force anything to its extancy. She curls over slightly, readjusting kinked tendrils by examining straightness of key. The road hollowed its location like gourd droppings treated chemically. Growth finally spreads inward to some handsome tendencies partnered by tread, in fascination, by love sandwiches.

A new way to watch time:

through fussy

fingers

& crystal sponging

or gleam of eye span

& succulence froth.

Vista backward is stretched to the root while recency sheds levels closer to the uni's core. We tap the common nail; we shatter grapes in harmony. The bread warms & protects its progeny; one leaf suckles the earth via stem & a trainful of liaisons approach endarchy.

[LINE: profession
pen line
road (map line)
border
underline
as in a script
a phrase or cliché]

Not a particular project is an "every," but this here I write. As I think bigger. A round up, whereas a flatter up would stick in applying to both surfaces. (Riding this domain sits taller on the saddle, but I tend to get stuck in particulars.) Homonyms threaten cuteness comma, etymology stings deeper, the flare of welcoming a certain arrival to the mind through the pen in mid-sentence. Like a note like this unravels. (Again, did the composer hear it first or was she the first to see it?) More like the knot "I was going to say." That man hardly, silly "stuck with" the name is one who has ravaged the sentence. You wonder about pillage, ravish & rampage, only to vanish back through the mirror. Thank You this & Thank You, them: does your mother's man plagiarize his forefather? This much deleted, why is concentration pointed rather than round? I think more easily spiral & the concentration accompanies the curve. Does a spiral palindrome truly go backwards or is there a hall of mirrors present in front of you.

Teasing the casual rewind into vibrant submission even pretends to paragraph, to play with enclitics, or graft via inverted "v."

It's the family metaphor rots, not the genus.

Women who call each other girls I call lady.
And am finally able within my aura, no longer enbarred.
I tie apples
I ring launder
I shy ratio
Elevate apple.

Highland possiblys
Frankstone watersense
Hyperhyphen dash dessert

Saskatchewan
One wan awone.
(*Popular quack jersey opening vinegar smashes. Sh'wishes she members.*)
The persistent basement dorm hall
The fire before the turtle
The broom closet.

Broom closet of articles.
Particles of speech
Dust & doomfall.

How cold is a bad experience?
Do questions evaporate?
Which end of the pencil is up to it. Waggling in his sleep, squeaky fon there, master green blows under. Answers expire.

My son is a mattress skier & a bed swimmer.

ONE CAN UNLEARN TAKING TURNING OVER FOR GRANTED.

> I call myself a dancer. I raise cattle, oats to feed the cattle, I slaughter, count heads, skin, dry & tan till leather for the perfect dancing shoes. I dye, design, cut, sew, don. Filing systems must be constructed to sort & organize the piles of material stacked & strewing the dancefloor: folders labeled, cabinets ordered, phonecalls made, worries pondered, rest & sleep, food & errands all facilitate re-creation of space via the removal of stuff. Years later, I come across filefolder of ideas about movement.

A seed for a fancy, & the gander borrows the voice.

I isolate further my nearest in her fancies. Eye for time, thirst for being. Peckled herself certain smiling through sleep breakers walk softly. Miles assured sail tenderly oven.

I wasn't capable of lazing. He wasn't culpable for lazy. We embargoed each either. A dream of the word "clash" undertaken overly abides no presentation. One letter wears under. Pressure trapped in eye.

A crispiness of sound undermines her complaints. Once this discussion of motes & billboards graffitied, of the laziness to pronounce, of the ease of hibition unemployed, everywhere they're telling us the page size before the idea even takes root.

We transverse a wooly terrain, free to suck in aridity. Set to undulate softly with or without, & eventually, the trio tuckers.

Opuntia pair double necked distraction honking goose horn finger fisted.

Lifter notion write out a truck's dreamland shrubscrub green & purple-brown emphatic.

An endorsing memory. Mammary grand and installing heresy in particulars.

Coasting eloquent, allergic to nothing, zoned & chewing or sparkle crackling little boy.

Oceans of dryness house grandstand opuntias, pap before percodan (& well before the following suffixes). Benevolent after the fact, violets & begonias violent but overwhelmed by a rhododendron spread. (p.s. – We can see in there, & sneakers of the same color backwards.) P.O. & a terse terrarium, snug glass wonderful putz by a gong asleep, roll tendency dormant.

The hall, life of sound & color in line : a wading.

Before what came the before:

Going home can be going home away from home.
Chicken, liaizon, "books," russia.
Mother be to myself larger family.

Home can be here can become before:

The essay on chronology veered backwards over the edge, would comparison dance with a metaphor? They'd love to. The face strikes the foot lash brow beaten tapestry symphony simply memory's molecule.

Turtlebrain swims succulent underground birds.

Sir Vivul?

Can't even hear the name.

FEAR?

Larger than capitals.

Polyticks?

Selfconscious unawaresman.

Titles. Don't always start in the same place, nor do sticks count to four here.

"Delivered Nunnery"
(Subtitle: A lark on the boom string)

Could gesticulate forward.
In terrarium delicious.
Every skininch "putchmy"
Silent gyration. G.I. ration.
Generation.
Uni- Nation
Indogent Diogenes.

[mathleth – to learn to forget]

Aggies in warrior country to the inside of making the playing creating. Gertrude Stein, where a mixmaster inward fingers the letter's handwriting. A mathleth of division, where a separation eventually accelerates growing. Look down to see the root-height's overlook if you're smaller. But he can't see the woods or the whole picture broadens for both of them. Only iterally. In seeing as knowing he looks, circumspect. Specs, drainage, hard plastic.

> There are bricks on a giraffe's skin, zigzag of mortar scales in baby felt the longer. I write the sooner son grows. Plants in the window before anti-gravity cactic mention in lax mind, lacks rhyme & language slacks into facts. Seriously growing onto timbre variation & lines run are pens watched their tips wiggle the boy wakes. Adding initials further teaches the music of memory heard the ear upon feeling. Dark wiggle, blink flickers.

Belly trap for green gushes nab me.
Sticking the thought inside the sound,
He noticed the shift; the pen stood.
Or green graces nail me.

Uneven light repairs the thought melted syntax moulds to tighten. Water breakdown thirty-two colored lights marched at the surface, shining up on top of other things, oftener than knots, secure in the sucking, k's incomplete, later wondering who or how long. Can the inkling chain? We are zoned out against the corner unloading a zest for rangers & isotopes. Each own fetish akin & forestalling stone faces out. Looking up, keep off the dunes. To clear of stomach on the chairs breaking.

Words trendy in a row more like chinese vegetables than mixed. Or styles jumbled, dryers & openers, three-prong translating back home. Pirandello grinds beans, bands & radio sweat, sacred thinking maybe books strained or connected passages, possibly both kinds of german glue. Like script or plastic over the crack.

All imaginable small mixtures or jar filters shelved one
oriental man after the another she held the door more.

The color of paper less obtrusive to words than the
rouser draws attention to Miekal's sword.
Cement snore:
Distracted by buying clothes
Distraught over holes in clothes
Colder than early april
Stunning of a farm.
Stylish allocations of primitiveness.

Verse toggle grates the cliffhanger's worry, the savior nearest church throttle, or interrupts a yearning. Tried & delivered the same tag yesterday at infant pasturing. Is this leaf an onions' remembering — dissolved or worm ridden, no mistake but first avenues coming again. Disassembled circles off railways & fear barreling faster, forgotten to tread long or thru icy's rideweight.

Tempering the ear tampers with word roots up thru the idea lane. Escalated urchin feather, I heard something, in Brooklyn thru France which fragment reminds you, a piece of discovery, the brain run by earthought makes beelines to theme rails.

Morals obtrude. Even metaphors slide. Gummed up sex, cantankerous longing. Machines love beauty & silence abides by nothing.

Church pickle.
Hysteria romp.
Why notitude in line for perfection.

That the pen could soothe so sooner. Rather deliver the pace of departure the fact "that" value tends to assert itself falsely. It rather innocently dons a moral cap, a capital letter, a belittling of the creative process, a guilt tease for reliability & her cousins.

> A new solitude uncovered, plain sheets & green colors. Don't give us to be fully of brandy. Or authoritatively besoin. Asleep on the axlerod gregorian planted & fessated was delivered & among. Free of book clutter I can read clearlier, sun floor at night pulls remaining garage.

Automatic door toy button pulley was wool fever & largo hymnic, mantagle & tunable histories. A is N in some triangles. Cliques rotate & translators leave town. Hypermaniacs transfer emotions at departure, while bargain luggage gets lost.

"Slaving over" is as unnecessary as shaving.

Frivolous urchins are padding in an essay, all-isotopes landed. "How's the rain?" House the rain, these pterodactyl spoons tiptoe the island over.

Sterility is bourgeois.

Hoarding personal masterpieces equals proudly databasing biographical largesse. Which words spelled differently suit the fairlane & tickle the dioceses.

The band snaps back to predetermined rigmarole when the cats flew. Jire jive handed the woodshed properly. And fairytales lie sleepily.

The pretension of the sophist made holy.
3 bottles left behind.
"Unconnected in *your* mind."
Disinformed or bottled slowly.
The perfect pen for writing handed.
"Just wait till he's three."
Tuesdays might.

Movements criticize critics who point.
The escalation of memory.
Sentences that are like nouns.
F-stops.
Short breaths.
Pearls strung.

Specialized familiarity. One good sentence makes the paragraph. The day shifted to gourds. Stops dead.

Idealized impossibilities.
Hopeful fortune subtle ties.
AB-SENSE.
How tripping could get you there.
Infamous stuck phrases.
Talking in regimented tastebuds.

Remedies for comma-tose ness include verbal fluidity, sea urchin exactness & a life of rally. Hup to oriental string teachers, plucked eyebrows returning home away from home.

How can I know who's talking if I'm not thinking while
I'm writing?
Or is talking a hesitation of the hand?

Infants are singing, simple verb forms ignored. Better to sit up, pass the juices, hold the bow, one hit will do. I'm:
fishing for the self.

Made her conscience against moving against myself. How can a hole hurt? He don't hold me. They haven't yet, so simply. Greens again fluttering, balking, melting in to. Filling in fallen out. Things heard not preferred. No one's fault that I apologize. Prepositions needed. We all were waiting on a line. Empty for juice, french for whole. Five? Grand. A night to leave for necking. Dangling participles are earrings for sentences.

Blocks. These plastic ones slip, & the air inside buoys against the structure of strength. Some build them & some get in the way. We even live on the smell of familiarity. The false tit, the beans outdoors but, the perpendicular one-way street. Cats. Even familiar one-word sentences. Dashing punctuation—stylish ties, heaven's postal link & copyists with babies. I saw on her desk the same share yesterday older beeping now replaced. Ours unpublished, left unique.

Blocks. Breakup with myself like some old friend, & shoulder the happening. I neither bounce off of him nor get discouraged. "You" could be "me" & better off is.

Is the pen as stick as removed
From the stalk of knowing
And the man "out there"
Included by walls

Renewed by-laws; the jargon runs thick. Last word on paper thousand "if" phrases or playing on old recognition.

"What is?" when there is more than the heart?
The pattern keeps sloping here, & the faces remain her.

Like a man I ignore the absence of women here
Like a woman I long.
Miso & Mauo, Momo & I say "picked apart today."

"Food express" is the ugly blaring attraction.
Away.
Back?

Out.
.Tangent
.Hinges
.Escapist
.Stuck tactic
Jealous of couples
Got me rattrapped like plenty.

Where's demotion?
Where's the beef?
Beef me up, make me stink
This beforehand
Always bad
Chutney pudding
Dressing bad
Mad ocean
Or timing elite
The sun flies crucifisk
Or softer pamby manitou

All hands on deck
A med-affair for seance?
More chutney in the offing

Ears hear in frequencies
Nose plotch forgetferble

An ancient ear

A corn pawn setting
Isle tendencies to member

Or rebirthing
Or foiling
He hears it
He runs it
It's his in the last place.

Old one ancient lecithin. If you looked up the uses charges would curl, each other passe no forgetfulness. Simplexity fluxus, not that turn on the faucet, necessity not hearing the script faster than heritage. Pen follows moonbeam past lighted viceroy, nor cars with women.

Not back in the cab in love with one.

You think I'm talking about *you*?

Instant-change-hot-goodbye-giveaway. Whatever is made stays but music glides in all directionals.

Two or three u-shaped things thrown onto paper in the memory of active partisociation.

Un o the next thing. My particular method was I just no writing. For merger, for "the millet's sun," was Zon little first or second time dotted the eye. Lost off a line's shadow. **Trying to think up tangled particle marsupials *too* can have humor milder than memory forked onto the edge of the sentence connected by little words & their children.**

Hard to believe you actually heard it, the chair breaking under the man sitting down. The device of the practical had never actually taken place, nor had the sentence straightened itself out. And then he's sitting there talking under the table slumps forward by step by step my jungle. Better than hugged up, ranting in line. Nor imitation hunger. He seating off the floor talking now; the novel fell the shelf. "Supper club," "limousine," "executive": "diarrhea" feels warmer.

DO WORDS SMELL?
DOOR SQUEAKS STEP
CAPITALS STAND UP

Lines ever grow. You remember it. Then you remember. Lines ever grow soft & the word has music, came home again, softened the sheet, that friendly public place, nauseous & inert, still still jagged arrangement yet coupled continuous. There ends what they ask me. The voice died, ear flooded.

When a machine arranges the page, the pen slows itself around a corner, tilted to hear violins roar. I'm smudging the runway by jolted passes. Huge open faces in the hills & half-third pink at the bluff. Glen water crinkles taste uncertainly.

How people in excruciating
transition look so alive.
Change is redder than green.
Stations or entry ways.
Words with jaw.
Flowing sophisticate without clothes.
And shorter terms cool the edge worth ten thousand

words
A faster imagery memo rate of change
the higher recall of mistaking a respelling for certitude,
in danger
or beyond this stutter.

The static is leaves from last nights shadow in tune outside the same book cover, this one.

I am of course writing with me in mind. Joshua ate the horse that bit his godfather.

Two stretchers giggle & turn out. Thanks again Gertrude. With bellies unturned, we lie again in mail between oceans of small cat bells singing the clichéity of the very word ocean has lost its scope. Polluted with material for ideas I eat citydust with opuntias in Larchmont. Where these places come from, I couldn't tell behind my shoulder with ants up the knee & the thought of doing any one thing even an eleventh that long.

He tended to get fed up with his own generosity once at each visit & twine on the way there hung sounds together & paintings up into glass walls incorporating thumbnails of nerve.
She walked in knowing full well, knowing. Pointedly jigsaw understanding a shot of fear originating in the belly of the head at a self abused dangerous sheer passing. Time to go in. A flow influence? Bar time, do it.

There's no end to this & more to learn on Saturday than the metaphor could push. EVERYTHING. *Everything* is included.

So happiness can't. So 6-year old pictures could relinquish wall space.

> *Plan tanes! With the nightperson oggle, my career church is hock! Balloons & lanterns, ice ex expressly. Parchment & chinamen, cinnamon sounds on brass oogling glens of beef & opped off dizziness with missing children visiting midwives themselves pregnant & walking into people, being given money & making no syntactical sense easily. Fashion on walls at eleven derelict pop. Jesus for the pen when eyes become ayes & all is eula. You There! Bigger than the paragraph starts & certainly adjusted with breaks & stops & familiarity.*

She notion the obsession in body orthology but note the selfsame baby massage communication. Ions for stasis. The broken heart menageried twirping twartling daring breaking awry or tawdry candle-ends split & burning. How melting is joining though heating churns fiction. Rubbing icons are ticklish. Even scrambled memories "set in," "spiral down," beers in the garden & okra for the allusion. A world without the. No quotes smell spaghetti or so healthy to run when away spins contusion. The bugs & ants of folks biking by at cooler head in the ground, sprouting heads from the ground. Opuntias punching words out leaving holes where prickers forget roses with father "in the garden." Became work as in at work not at it but serving other on their time off not usually writing but some thinking harder than thanks for Virginia's advance but Gertrude's kick. Without people the cows are soft & empty, the restaurant shut down, clink of glasses, "all gone."

The need for new punctuation unruled & unruly.

Getting used to an age group is two clichés soldered by two & wondering later where the el sound went. (This is this is.) Even clichéd discoveries while wishing to not recognize the piece of the bar's song across the street. It makes hurt sense which only the line & the spark obscure.

when the head
ignore the other
members

Painted for shirts sale hole in the table off ramp combination. Paired with coupling & octave spread. Wrung & spinned, rung & spit.

What is counting when lovings not tracing. Fire & over the church, able. Looking out while down at one time in two times. Picturing smile out at turned down eyelids unclosed & bowed. As in brackeous not extenuated.

Favorite old words out of their chairs, sharing the night air. Not enough twisted. The inside-out turning of the written tongue via little replaced or removed. "Particles of each": common frasis later.

INSIDE WRITING. With the foot clicking, something's coming out. She's flue of the table. Nascent & able. Lovetripped foreign kisses & babies bright-red-little-lights-in-a-box. Gray plastic, water-people in the other room running reverse of the weave is color busy with fraying.

I'm writing on towards every. Burse fanny gtting ovfre gt gvtp (Little) Saint.

Though heavy to hang east, jewel therein a sign. "...there on the street, thas werew she gtin" Tranceshock his breathing mercury history sound forked in a turning over for a hundred works about one verb. Not love as it is able, tripping further the unasked transmission arrives, welded. Falls wear off. Where screams are screeches clucks crawl into a painting. I can't figure to break contractions. These are passage connectors so beyond their home, words even as to stagger u to stagger apart, *should* spring out there, back & with ease, whether I trick myself into language or it to me. Slanted on tin penline nuggets, nasty general. "Glad for this," the punishment shifts into magic.

Liquid gem makes peeps in the night. "Quantum Fatherization" renewed 6 mos later, loud on the shelf. Fear of Fear is in your head. (Better to talk to her self than the other)

Yesterday's booth was rattle & flair & languid & icelandic. I urchin the fantastic her pen shake. The syllables as I reach that place where it can't stay the same let the painting break; let the rats emerge. Immergency, a one by one allowing entrance only forward mixed brands in holding back. What we are writing about here. Which line in to slow it down? Restraint of circular. The physiology of the relationship. How two blocks shutter down unshared rivulets homeward.
Our.

Rapidly I steal the territory of my thought or whose hands built the raisin's distraction: A flight against automacy as in automaticality.

> The young lady stoops to pick up the dime & thinks of a reaching in the middle of a month long day. This reminds her of the hill in a dream sitting next to a brother's thinking. Shaping huge stone, inventing lists, & lists of inventions, these & the musics, even glistening interruptions & neck gray noodling——all on paper, the book all in capitals.

The minder slower than it ramble, but cute little butt actually "good sized" talking a sentence of them there: the candle began to shake an earthquake. Turtles & butts & heads of babies boobs. The mark that vanished before appearing red down the alabaster's brow.

Weaker between passages, lighter when under construction. Limited by page size & pen motion but freed in front of a screen. The sparkling eyes finger tiny royal bronze pillows shaking in the box. He has the power to free them. "I don't have to accept it, you know." And the scar never shows, but she boasts.

COCKROACH sanity desktop underwear icetray coming lake water simultaneous sighing & silly, alphabet-free lucky underlay. We, we trespass.
MYSTERY cloggages, history of lost miles & gentle arbitration grazed leaning of rail rays, women of clothing or ice-handsome backstrength varied at crooked engine.
ALIVE fearness looked in the other eye or tasted the underside or dropped home stunting when surprise swallows kick down & siddle over.

Times writ & the canaries will isolate their fantasies' mercantile adverturesome workguests or ordered pigstock for fancy. Prices laid or confusion connected. Ding dong the ferry! Ice tentacles for jubilation undergrowth. Rising-ask-crackers spinnet or ferret all faster the fatter dreams of tents & limits, buckets & jerkdrowns for the mongers chewing, inventories typed, arhetyped or slated free. **Can you trapeze my terrarium?** Isn't really a zoner but glides like the ferris. Trenches rethreaded. Rock stops along the way, cynical redhead or puffy-eyed program coordinator pressing keystones for derringers. Agnes was right there in the book laden feathers. Happy glockenspieling, thanks to translation, the cheeks full tilt listen their rightly.

SHADDUCK! A hair torn sister shiver fishy modernity knitting of a sailor worst turn by angst towers hung gourds spiral clinging for wurst lover foley.

Mill talk.
Harper's dune.
Clip farber.
Herpe's tale.
Iceman cow-if.

Jester deepers
Tuned fanatic
Dripmore clingant
Fuzztone canary
Solitary why
Slaphappy pencils.

Cardboard outside, elephantine ursala upsalla upsidedown, lift blowing frucus originator lost track of the round thing not circular motion. Tense justification. Flows. Hirt. Daundry. Lent. Earstress. Disinfact. Harpy delearnium.

Peat Za.

Isotomes & catacombs
And culinary arsonpatch
Each topographic catastrophe
Plate.
Solo-breath unsituate.

The female pincers lie straight stout & close to one
another:
the male more slender & curved to pinch."

Which openended stutter can't explain itself?
Is each night's worth just for the book at the end?
Does the end versus the ending?
Peat moss tragedy.
Burial tooth.
Icicle Footsy
Elephant sheen.
Ejaculation graduation.
Younger than centuries.
Lip service to hunger.
Farmer nothing.

Out of clay, for the corner of a room painted gray.

Brainstorming the catacombs of a complex universe, minds sally under tradition. Transluce overage swallows moonfuls & patabons of first taught flavor-obvious slanderies the pen ear churned forward. Ice cubes in milk, hairs on tits; "the brain can't really talk for itself." Since only one kid knows nostrils, will she remember it matter? Which thing can't be done without the other.

Barely covers the flavor cold.
Is a head there not eating.
VW has its letters.
Others do so.

Women's phrases. The eagles' ranting verses discriminate intellectual varnish. Transylvanian cattitude. Purple luxury tentacles & watermarked swords, diamonds & verdant places, mistaken tokens, back of heads muttering the secret "quickchange" philosophy of cool air. Shady reference here today, when ice works differently in milk. The warmer the conjunctions the faster the eating. Cloaks of speech. Hung my memory? Imagery agog after the fact.

Backwards goes baldheaded lady the Not Quite.

She doesn't move the tendency to dawdle from the perspective of confusion.

The tower is clouded over, its fire smokeless. This much seriousness needs some water, that brand a foothold. And the brass rings. Sweet face concentric opposity corroded & foolish ears examining backwards. The cool moon's road walks into gas smells & coke. Ug where blood on snow is more naturally hued the irony takes on a sin. Terror-shadow of missing man missed dry water or buried deeper. How the troubled are the troubled ones. You're never surprised. So the critic isn't a man & she forgot the love at home and left behind herself. The smaller the word loaded, even feistier than text pellets clicked & placed. Pixel-dragons step? Medievalty cut in line for anachronist plagiarism.

When the flow's done the ear grabber cuts in, down the brain hums sliteyed shut down slid "oofta" without being thaught it. The newest word is up because faces are of pants & on legs, & parts are described by parts built in context in concept inconsequential.

Some of the slowest mouths aren't connected to their brains which run more multi-smoothly. A master juggler of words sat speechless to say them but the record of his motion astounded. Bewuttled backness into dreams into undescribed otherness back to faces facing me with true speech & young cow eyes.

The old hag returns, asks where the devil now sleeping.

Loosen it from the inside & it will come out.
The more important it is, the more distractions in other directions, leading to knowledge of trails tailing dichotothot.

New sentences,
dead plants,
clean floor,
composition,
zon's face,
constructing steps,
preparing heat,
money & numbers,
sharing a goddess
computer percussion
ankle massage

crisp realization
positive inkling
comfort enables
nut butter sedates
almond indifference.

This break mead the hearing the fourth time more than a quarter different. I hear Karl hammering, filing, rasping, sweating, though the composer speaks coldly of conducting. Conducting heat, he thinks. It sounds like there's an order.

(Subtitle:) This Backspace Won't Delete.

Foreign language still requiring distance, the double stander took the wing himself & flew for a roll. "Casual at first," this cool word clucks familiar panties at a torso. The oddball turnabouts & black to white flounces, the flicker of emotions & subtle variables all dynamite & tenderness——ah, welcome, this, welcome uncertainty, candor, & eros. Twitch me a good one, laughter fatigues only patience already thinking too ahead.

As if capitalizing edifies, once in a while you strike. Connected by corners, filled in on the same level, this language can only cement. Bungling left or right bumble. Bumbling right or left bungle.

NO fear, snakes through their homes are nursing him to dark. Hints sound to accompany a listening beyond the stone voices. Shoke the other side.
NEW lines take off where old ones ended but not when. After & at the circle's recognizing itself as a hole.

TASTE the parchment. Be athenealit preternatural. Colts with numbers at least reremembers.

Impossible wanting the cherry taste with mount closed. Strings attached to the lines' curve cry to be sung but the lovely singer's hairs need washing, so the concert doesn't—— Dashes stand behind tooler toiling without lifting chair or isolating movement. Ran out of time tolerating. Impossible situation started up again armed with conscientious hibernation shifts never mention pain-clear turtle visions respined.

Clamp stomp preceded by a simultaneous moth wishing an introduction, categorical continued writing, dead colors lower in voice, & a message remembers. Parking lots are private risings of rock reverberations crawling hug slabs & bass memories. (The e returns)

Bits have left the hand-out table for loaded little units which be mere dots if someone hadn't pondered it long enough. DENY NOTHING. She blodded out gray NO's capitalized not to be numbers alone but onesies seriously healing.

The meat of existence found at the sexual market gives pen to spice & back again. In line, each shelf opens up; not only little ones hold tight. The goddess cuts her own hair just in time for the feast. Life support systems buried & thrown over the edge come full circle only when stimulated full. Fill in the blank lanes with sandy tracks while rethinking this metaphor:

SMOKE GOD.

Leak opens. "Sha," it said. "And" through Dee-En-Ay makes

dan "quake."

Will the wound feel good this time? Find me me. Set forward woman also teases inspirchange. Everyone opens. May up continue also be out. And wait again. Still. Be still. Slower sex. And faster sexed after.

Just because it wasn't done earlier? Exclaim! Fucking few women lustloft the obscure. Her name? "B. Sexish".

As eye I it,
B SEXISH,
the woman my mother wasn't & is.

Some space left around the hole. Think, the fall. Leaning on capitalization to skirt the severity of it. I am free. To joke the baby for sale likens it to a walk through more than one state. Up across & down la rue. The curcubated mind flies renewly tabbed & multifixeted. Offish, temple grabber! Spe, Spe, self-smirking. Ha! in print, already here! Waiting working waits, poor sexish states, "ha." Oar the edge I needn't plagiarize he naren't follw. We nossilish arem.

Viqrant feszich orptril klmetr.

RESURGE
recent
refile
reimagine
re originate
re order
re pocket

referent

I wore a black bra over my language in a recent effort to refrain from reaching for regular formulas, a tongue-fall of depression, light transient windfull reversed in odoured tieframes. She wins out so is untied.

Ice pickets parlay aptly a river over gigantic truss.

Random clothing changes the tempo, forged in ink to suit the gander.

> Cam jemila, tentacles rearing indeficient political
> siamese confession = two-headed turtle sense.
> Pasta kookoo person not changest the irai level gesto.
> Reshaven
> Reshaking it.
> Residue titanium or raucous erupt.

Persona not thinking colloquial at gratis station paring churchbells with telepathy geared for statuous grog-range purses lipped ejaculate danger seat zone under transparent glee causes or rhapsody larynx tractor. Rintintin first favorite anything tri-escalated & shaven further. Duckmesticate lien tablets bouncing shrilly, regard of all mycenae, or tangents mapped out customarily hand done & drawn back to let the sun out which once in scorched his scenery blank (et).
Brilliant transgression jive-right similarity.
"Your sly shows up on paper"
Chamomile sedates, she gave him doses for a dollar before the quotes fell off. (And coming off is always more entertaining.)

When & if the woman ever delivered or ordered this explanation undertaking to trespass her original right & convenience to quabble whatever ways. Round open shred to rocky heights. Climb the barrio, trace till the millionth.

Xabbi boned to freezer undulate indirect perpetual mind display. Urchin keys wandering grace recital, all selected under efficient inexact triumph, recurs in each act. Particles ice the wave, template forcer drawn across the verbal possibility, better through than thrown away, when ice churches equal 3 times the drum cleaner.

En why. Coded geography. Autobiographical playing with itself. Coated: each action overdressed with so much worried preparation as to be stuck, stiffed. Each breath is there that could be a "creation" deadened by ignoring, charged later in a looking heightened by remembering realizing one thing about large span of past, clouds between the spiders & the present rendering of a fly's poke in mother's wing. Past psychology to the warm huggableness, broken on to humming about computer-thinking, then re-rendering the ineptitude of the pen.

To catch the mammaries in opened mouth as quick as they fall while assimilating the feelies they evoke (and certainly too the words, certain verbs living with certain nouns, tied in a overdependent but sensible pair), a couple expects until the watch stops & the car is left unlocked inside the underground garage.

Clean events eventually clean up after themselves, while dirty evenings chide. He zigjogged through the horns blaring to the clunk the heat turns on just as at home in another city, remembering fitful dreams. I can't tell when the ice controls but, three pens past the palladium the baby scrambles. Kicks crotch a two-step on thick carpet after a day in the sweat. A third lane above the arm saves the taxpayers plenty. A penny for tea revving up the brain. Works eloquently, diverse works, works in a restaurant. Works well under water.

That a body could take precedence over the things that it does. "Are you going to give up for these 3 years?" How one can smell the temperature of the rain. Who could sit at a box for hours. The fingers are still ignoring the back. How too much leads to "the simpler things."

How when you travel you take yourself along but not your studio. Pieces of paper. She had never thought of this, in someone else's office are no threat nor distraction.
How he plays with her shoe & would never do that to me. Nor do I moan beside myself. When the scope fills up, my brain rattles, beans for business, a little of everything for later. Where do you wanna grow, little boy? We're psychoadaptable, virtuostic luxurates. Oh, do me but leave on the next boat, get out. The can't-have is luscious. I'm crazy.

She lovely does look like a boy. And that boy, I tried to end with a comma, but it kept giving on. Agracadooche!

The sumptious undertoe is uncertain-sexy. To match the everhard with soft big brine would ecstatic too much but to dream. Dreams don't touch the trip in the closet darting faces teasing flipped about, the Japanese beauty tough out of her culture, miles from the tongued traveler. Is it the skirt or the issue? (In a row of Christian lights at the edge of my distraction, one stands above the others & I am immediately knowing it's me.) Dressed just like her, I am nonetheless taller with these sticks in my hand. I couldn't resist the comparison: What's the history of black; the otherness inspires me, one touch lost.

Eyeballs jarred, one after the other. Turned back, upped it, close the twist stunted by type torn from waiting, backed out. Is hex-noise leans a screw. Padded, left behind, she jolts the particle. A torque to do it reminds of moving, fingered eyeless. Islets eyelids "Isa" pronounced "blue ball," coughs as if color unallowed. He ya! Chaotic psychotic, the rhyme removes one, pops its belly, crisp ooze: the mind inchoate. IN CO-HATE. *Sexed opposition eclipse.* Nauseous turbid.

All these girls feeling funky are tight forgotten, to which add the afterbrain of forethought & you wonder which wind is blue. The same with muscular high tails or anyone's butt. Whispers. Moistened opened.

THWARTED. A glove in wont of a hand.
A high wasted.
A mountain with outlining.
Anger
Oppression is power bottled, labels mocked,
words tossed askance.
Switching roles is learning.
Feeling is painful.
Loneliness shared by every man & woman.

When eating the other was forbidden I built closets & sucked in them. Now that the door is more or less open, I set a duet so strict I nearly starve him. An indigenous diet, staying home.

April 1993

Every Lines Other

Language

Is this the end of the line? The palm-line of doing being, breathing beading. More lessening. How the train has to stop to let you on. Hummer. Short spurts in a long symphony. Objectified is a goddamn verb. With or without the N, the family name, the sixth places names the key. Who would have read it? That the spinal potential is as negatively charged as the brain, except when asleep. "We're talking" reversed parenthetical assumptions: Here, that that many spirits can so radically exchange up the front line.

These months of dormancy have given me much to last in. If only the manner were as speedy as the tumult raging & raining to be let out without cluck-start pause – squelching the mucus back in choked pieces even the handwriting begins dancing the computer flashing red lights "the sheet, the shirt" isn't that at a different café? Going back to the writers, the readings, and after reading, reading. Traveling before traveling, so you can be going somewhere. 200 year old orgies.

Full circles now are full of big wars, future war, & people healing themselves & each other, everywhere love. Seriously, & needn't slow down to shore up. Treading to these who can think writing to she who remembers to breathe: calm, rainingness, and too much muscle. The variety of passion are matching clamshells, biorhythmic dessert.

Language/Diary

The globe is inside of me now, beginning to, We love our voices & our words. We dig holes & later well up with desire, candid about our own clichés, habits finally hugged as rituals, others already bit. Always a humor in sense, you write your understanding along the way, simpler, simpler, you whirling dervish me, I can feel it on my nipples, both of them outward like the hotel building at the water.

Scrawly mobile now, remembering longing laster. Hesu, a reversal of polarity back to normal right before the change. chaos precedes order: we learned that at the beginning of the river. To pine is to. Proliferation of gourds like leathery animals everywhere, sleeping for now & breathing. So.

Big shells were almost scary, the animal they are a house for. If you chop up a line & read it in pieces you get a feel for its circular continuum. What's wrong with this sentence. The tricks of scientists who write.

I eat facts instead of cookies now, since I don't author texture. The jinx rabbits, the phalanxes coming out of nowhere, the tipsy ventriloquist funny enough to be nauseous—— Belly's aching are better than clichéd overusedages. All english becomes a disgusting cliché, as if it weren't yesterday, my pen follows the synapses. Not just using their vocabulary now but really conducting connections through & around the new terrain, into the gut & our my cunt which is more mine now & his is slower.

Language/Diary

Anything ends the sentence. Everyone begins a line. I love. If my flute were here, it'd be a drum.

No noise, no plants, no dirt, no disorder, & yet I love my mother

especially when she's sleeping & can't smell my feet. You like comedy? The dirt that gets between us has to smear like shit, you know, so we can both smell it. I sound rowdy & frizzed, riled at
this history that hollowed out women.
Which impulse ends up in the feet? Ions parading. A see-through walkway around the village, a hill so flat you don't see you're up. All directions analog human. Rhyming heat with meat is riskee for a three year old who drinks before sleep.
If the readers know each other that well after so many ears do the metaphors too transparent & the mannerisms bare? Can I ask them rather than read? Is this for them or for my crotch? We don't dare get titillated but we can't help it. Mothers of mothers finally glad for entropy, it happened so fast.

Sex
("Stringing, chunking – it's like oxygen masks going on & off, blinkin ivy's telling the truth, snapping desire comma after coma wetter than an onion. We lick each other regularly, she said, but no one really knew whom she referred to. Openinger & openinger. Just shows to go to english stop signs translate endlessly all using the same hand forward.
Oh got transparently egging, your industrious covering lovette.
Sashaying, a word I'd never ordered until him. Days later, under extra covering, we thinking them us.
Somethings radiating. Spoiled by an asterisk reminds me of beans in his kitchen. Going by too fast to throw them away.
Split so many ways she's her own sexy stranger.
Feeling what it is my hands want to be feeling while making, or drumming, ——writing includes more so I pen-dance, try to, stumbling heart pump. You get older, you're more direct. You

humblize then trip over an immense young body. Chaos in children in numbers. Finger-pointing or on automatic. I am nauseous from not. We can sense things, & we write of "we" now, an older council, in conference. At age, we convene. Austerity, gray gills. commas of period. And sexier, little do the younger know. I love you on an airplane. Dedifferentiation. Not just stripping but starting anew. How stuck in pronouns, gender, syntax & cadence. Up off, "oeuvre," "dehors" et "sorti a," that gets things moving.

Visual Language

Intelligence is wholedness.

Challid, Allah, challis, trellis, Hollis, won, one, honey, horny, quincy, mincemeat, tenderizer, self-derision, indecisive, intersection, intercision homoerectus, perspectus, Persephone, Hermione, & cacophony; heroine, capacity, horrible capricious, hair cap, have not, hairnet, hornet, hornier, fournier, Gourier, Robbes-Grillet, grilled rabbit, triumphant heroic, recovering heroaddict, rectangular reaction, read action juice, gist, Gish, dish, Seussing, loosing, s or long z-ing, Ping! As one word only: drumstickockaos.

Bravado, ignoramus, ignore the puss or drink it.

Hire the man or pinch him.

Hurt the lair or maim it.

Hiram bland nor Maynard.

Brilliant *perpendictions*, parallel pricks asses everywhere. This woman's muchness deserves its distractions which are multidirections, & rathers than not-heards. (Every time I think too hard a dream memory turns on then short circuits.) Trusty glands, secrets, land deep hurts or deep loves. Sexiness crossing over love in the act of massage. How the writers sit

down day after day, & the sewing machine is always set up, the paints always out, the sarcasm of telepathy. Must my pen itself be drugged? People people "your new addiction?" I hope you're addicted to living well but don't see it as a problem. Recovery is a tool, don't dangle on it. Sympathy nor pride, I adore you stage. Sympathize in my shower, horny, & speak French on me.
Walnut catnaps.
Two words.
Brefity.
Extra salamander arms.

9-7-95 thru 10-7-95
Every Lines Other

Visions

The goddess is holding a question-mark of dripping blood.

A gigantic fire-breathing toad.

A diamond-studded gray leather corset-belt around my waist, sexy surrender.

Smoke trailing along a wooden floor out the back of a flowing satin floor-length dress.

A porcelain glazed picket fence, "fire red."

Eddy & airplanes.

Snakeskin spread-eagled & glistening translucent in the sun.

The air inside fire.

Big words on a page, meaning small words in big type across the page.

The black x's on shiny tin drums & soldiers I must have nightmared about as a child.

Apostrophes & commas dancing parallax past each other, in the same direction, just out of sync.

Zon's flip-flops, marbles, sand, & sticky suckers on a stick, not necessarily in summer.

Hair parted on the side.

Salamanders.

========

Diary
The pregnancy of road gas tends to twirk the memory glands or marriage predicts a contagion of possible certainties. And, certain ties tug at the tangents of love bubbles we simultaneously prick. (Do we write in order to fill pages or empty hearts? Get it out, but form the stream carefully, with pursed lips & rounded holes. I sing my body eclectically but "because of outgassing it was described as tenacious outbursts, extraneous noodling behind tendrils." I've learned since to suck it in down to the bone. From the bottom up cleaned & clear of all that isn't all that is left. The minimal possibility went untended for years of unstacked hay piled randomly in sense-balls & lined up in trivia-rows. Whose inner voice is this? Whose inner child? Am I pregnant? How full can a beautiful woman be, if it weren't for triads, nodules, & corpuscles? I'm sick to my innards watching out for expectations, looking for small white cars, waiting for something if not nothing. Going from hard places to soft in a shine!

____

____

Language
When language can flow like the body, breathing out & in & out, angels stand like children being, words grateful for music & fingers dancing with marker. Language elevates; music enervates. My English teacher accused me of being nervous; I taped drums & danced before I knew it. I'm beginning to prefer English for documentary purposes only. I.E., I close my eyes for a vision, then write it here:

AN EYEBALL OPENING TO REVEAL A THROAT OPENING

To reveal a friendship, *feel* the clock. Nervous boy, naughty girl. Pesky fly, danged money. Jointed splitter spits out numbers. She adjusted the weights after her ride ended, assessing burn marks & other hopeful scars. She alludes to her friend in France, her friend *from* France, rolling down the histamine, toddling to herself, jogging sluggishly before she picked up speed. Past, present; left right, gauche adroit. Swing long enough & you complete a circle. We're laughing at the language – it wears mamma's pants, pretends to be so advanced as to translate, correlate, & *relay*. Language without music needs the crutch of imagination or various tools like space, paint, keyboards or the perfect pen.

* * *

!
Good numbers come in small bunches. Batches of red chunky liquid waiting for words on their jars while reminding us of home, of hearth & heartiness. Looking forward to breath we can see, anticipating each other's snow-crunch. We pulling

up blankets to chins only after knee joints bend delightfully loose. They sneak away together behind her own back. Back in, sense travels in circles. She's happy to adjust, considers it a challenge to survival to balance mid the chaos. Her lens is focused & focusing.

. . . .

Language & Diary

I'm telling birds to shut up, and there's no way you'd know what I'm saying if you didn't know Ariel & Dizzy. Numbers are music to my ears as well as dots are equal to lines. Every line's other. Add the "ess" to our daily utterance, "oh my" dot dot dot. Birds needn't such trivial exclamations. Because I'd rather write. Step up. Step in line. Save space later. Each moment hides embedded in this bed of words on an imaginary page (one of language's biomes.) A diversity of functions is fulfilled in the chaos-flow of my dance with thought with pen. (Ariel is nibbling my chin, sucking in my heat?) Why do I write? To document a flow, a song or story of my various positions & interactions in the flow of time. (The bird is in my face.) "This is crazy." To notate the sounds in my head (languaged music). To write a book by October 7th. To enter fall properly, on the couch. Writing as a seasonal leisural. Essay, to write about. (In french, "easy" "enough.") Painting whole pictures. (Dizzy said "broken eggroll.") The yoga of drawing? No, yes the art of sentences. Thoughts have their own *feeling*. Like the feel of "parrot talk" versus the feel of the thought of Eddy. (Some sentences are connected.) Some ask for veils on one side or the other; I only wish parentheses were asked to be paired. "Purgatory pie," she sighed. "Butt liver" might be remembered for Miekal's tone of voice, more likely "Chicken Butt." Where the reutterance becomes crowned by capitals. Big letters on a small page. Capitals immortalize & sharpen, point to & point out. I feel important enough for capitals. (Look under "Character.") All right, hot dog? Cheap words taste just as foul. "I'll write two more sentences & when the page is full I'll stop." What's the white space in the permaculture of writing? Certainly not the lawn. The soil? Tabula rasa.

Help!

Send me to the basement & flush me out.
        Flush me full of wet, my lovely.
Over shore certainly, I heighten to totally.
        I feel unto me, I of you
    with itness in sexy words.
(Where it touches. She rotates to the book
        (or I'm ricocheting elflettes.))
    The tong unwhittles itself with him,
my overloadly, a story comes on:
- - -

Years ago there were lasers, big fat razors of rind & tremolo over icers & bicycles on tin raymond dungaree elders. Berries with wigs or fat, & sprigs of earthware planetary dragons whose charm were in their whiteness & the purity of their beige. Ivory plastereds for buxom raincoat fairies twirling & tittering at me sing twelve graes for the day-fall.

A dainty enters. Her teardrops glide in to goldness

shafting me awake. Clearly, freely, I stagger upwards, shoop-de-doop. Ever languid et dangereuse, the very limits of language masquerading as sense gives me license to hear all as music. Blatantly spunky language spits me out spits fully; where's my left rein? Sliced open, fallen into, so stung it's deluscious.

The soft one lies out her every, look.

Looky *there* the words are sexy, think of Roland Barthes. (Sandi says, "Please, can't we call them something beside "the French people?!") Of course they know Artaud, he wasn't pronounced properly.

How stuck can an obsessing get? The lean tough cat slips in the room & I lick butter. So stung it's delicious. I full it.

Dream

The parallax universe pulled up last night in horns. They were paired with mirrors, though the shade of pink was more purple. I took a long breath & my time opened up. I stood on the corner of a lemon cucumber while I reminded herself way into the future what time of year it was in the story: time to ask Sandi about the sage or see what was smoked.

The Cave

It's damp down there, but I keep forgetting it's warm. Warm damp moists. Disease-houses happening, bargains change. Fungus eroticus. (He could arrive at any moment.) (Fragments of the future "fuck with" my self importance.) Think of the detailed ones, the couch-washers who lost the forest. My mother emptied the ashtray after I ate its contents. I am lame-dazey in dithers here, ending in ditches but forgetful of the damp earthenware steps down, downward. Downward

I step, one step & another, down, down & dripping & warm & luscious intoxicating down there surrounding me & erse me. Immerse INTO, steam follows, the air is clear. An underground hot spa cave for I alone. I can let no one in, it won't exist. Definitely a lion in there, the panther still lurks. Snakes & toads & sweet water-rats murking. Come in with me, my sweet? Appalled in another zone, I take "him" unto me. I suck & re-use the image like a soggy cardboard mask while I dare myself to break free. Puff it up with perfume, exhalterate trop daily. Yeti, I remember. Yeddy she hides him, tomes she could confiscate. Help, send her down there, or out to the garden, & down from there through the burdock. Dig down down where it's bitter cold. (Before she imagines further, into the lava beds into the fire that's so tempting, so sexy as to inflame you, no joke of a matter, you can't belittle an element with words...)

How can I struggle duly with music melded to words here, — frumpy dumped on English, like it's the only voice. Kids whine parrots screech hump my horn or get the phone, "It's her boyfriend, the small white car." A huge funny metaphor is embarrassing on paper. (This is the kind of thing I won't remember having written a week later.) You can tell I'm off-loose. My balance is staggering between dexterity like a juggler & the way out there in the avant noise planet putting it to words. (How personal by example of the word "mode" with a fake Bohemian household in a big kitchen I masturbated in for a year///

VISIONS

1. Net over a square hole.
2. Toys underwater.

3. Projector burn-mark.
4. The sound of the word "donut" with a giggle.
5. Venetian blinds accordion-folded.
6. Slipping leaning sideways.
7. Bowling balls, fingerholes at top.
8. One wool sock in the drier. Dryer.
9. A pear-shaped light-yellow light-green natural light source.
10. Orange & yellow striped paired rays of light or railroad ties emanating from far space.

Sex diary/Language/Story

I sneak lines here & there: I'd rather be stealing kisses. More important to caress myself. She reminds her of the map of her intending. The way things are lining up tightens the equinox out in the dark of the moon. Watch her holler, trying to forget herself in motion-laden desirings, feeling cells pop & quiver & shift & shivering them out in words on this page till the monkey come home starts teething. "Scratch me," the alchemist begged and with the other hand cracked the beaker tighter till it drew thick drips of blood down her hand. ("Now you're talking," said the publisher, when really the action as she knew it was preceded by the feel of the memory of an old image re-drawn.) "Chew on that." He offered a nutbowl of glass shards. "Delicious," she deceives him: "Look behind the curtain." She veils her disgust with a smile & turns toward the door. He can wait no longer so begins to write the novel.

Story

The other one, the younger one, enters the scene like a smooth black cat & starts clawing his way up the drapes to the ceiling. Her tongue reaches up & out of a. (Glitch.) She turns to aim it at the solid one. "I'd like to put a line on you." She threatens with upturned eye & brow in a frenzy. She almost attacks but instead turns to the cat asleep on the couch & pets it affectionately. "I admit I can enjoy the twisted nature of any whole situation," she announces, & slips back to her former self. She weighs in just right then & snaps back into the ring & there's the feather again, smaller but brighter & deeper orange. Kitty opens one eye & is upon it. He's viciously playful as it transforms bird-wards, a pet for some split seconds, but then she grabs him. Hard, from behind. "Tighten your language for me," she grips. "Harder," he begs. "Better," she allows & licks his entire back in one swoop. He disappears again, less like the Cheshire cat than a restless teenager. So she turns her attention back to the armchair. Something in it gristles.

∞ ∞ ∞ ∞ ∞ ∞ ∞ ∞ ∞ ∞

Breathing Visions in the Cave

Wet black, like living velvet endless deep pool. You have to immerse in the cold dark water & swim deep underneath for just longer than your breath can hold till you reach the underground fire. There the water bubbles up warm & soothing & you can have animals with you now, one or two. Lick each other & play lightly; smell the pollen in the air. Plants hanging down grab you with succulence & you realize that, finally, you've forgotten. You know what it is that you have finally left behind but still now you've crossed a threshold & you can look at it lying there & it's all okay.

//

Tempting experimental, I test clarity over the richness of cloud formations. I take focus & hollow it out. I thicken lines to see if they clarify like butter. I allude to whey when describing elixir.

The liquid I generate takes time to sweeten, several rounds before it clears. I'm drought-resistant but suffering from the heat. (Metaphor is too easy, a trick with no meat; I question myself but remain mute.) He takes me to visit the mill again & again I return a year older. Nonetheless, the twins felt comfortable with her double life.
How many mirrors deep can we go?
X X X X X

Visions
Visioning the coming winter...

Wood. Fish. Light.
Silver horn. Melting sex. Healing belly.
Lonely warmth. Warm mouths. Gold blanket.
[Slanted steel beams. Hot new music. Sweet smell of grim.] (A trip to the city.)

Diary/Sex
Arid until you share shock: computers are generating honey-hives, executive combs, lowflying air-laughter, & hellacious muffin affrontery. Stop! Push it! Do now, do hard, *get there.* (The farther in & out there I go, the more English fades away. The music is screaming, the music says, "Say me!" The joint of the silver horn finally joins the silken back. Black hair & horn players together like a pair of dreams. Shut up & trust it.
Hone up I'm in it.
Hose off with me, over there.
Taking them with me while I take it off, I wonder why I can take it, where my mothers wings come from, why the treachery's unfolding. Listen stronger I tell me, breather & tolerate. Isn't

the music meddling with the coronary harm felt underneath the vestibule? I venerate venerate: this "year" I found where the "x" meets. The sock's off the under toe, hadn't I noticed? Open the bottom petals to the earth. I come, offering sweet elixir – clear like broth, of darkness borne: Cherish this. Or burst the infinite. Listen for the motorsounds signaling the end of the dizzy-romp in the worldheadspace & pipeladen fantasy hampered by body-sit language in sexhell. The writer is preparing for out-of-body travel. She gets in the vehicle and then, she gets back out again. How a simple sentence can cause a shift. (I'm not inspired, I'm obsessed.) *I write because it's a very sexy act.*

ooooooooooooooooooooooooooooooooooooooooooooooo

Diary/Sex

My green pants smell like goat's milk I can't write fast enough to catch my train my thoughts race rattling swirling into & out of their own circles I sway sexy in them, brandishing doubt, tripping over guilt, ice skating through my own history – fudge, fright, or factors other. The other one. The "other" line. Our otherness. She zigzagging evermore faster than her foot she flexes her angle she puns all too oftly self conscience without the "e". "ELIXIR" she dares to write – Truth or Dare (before she reads it.) What present for him? Always & very near every other. Remove, remove. Breaking stone, feeling *under.* Grip under. Trance myself *out of*, ask not to doubt. Cry *into it.* Fuck the publisher, kicks the guilt out of the way. Scary lonely scary uncertain and certainly free. Lix leaps the dark chasm, then breaks out of sorrow. Tomorrow the mail-lady comes. She's wearing a silk skirt & her face grins familiar knowingnesses at me. (Where am I going? Can I get there any faster?) She's out of her gourd & she likes it that way. Let go, let go of the reins, ——Let the bottom drop out! Dark dank deep deep water take me I go under. Bury me I melt myself, deigned to lick my own mucus tract in unedited simplicity. I feather lightly this little flicker my only womenly, glorious to be out of my mind, ironic: I lick myself with my own words of freedom, as if I had the game undone, where my worst enemy is my restriction. Some people slow down for the handwriting; she makes belief of her onliness. I'm shocked at the volume of flow, now that I'm full. I let go, I heal, I cry. I shiver, I scrawl, I indulge according to the publisher & I don't care because I feel it in my tits. A sick sexy suitor, a girl in a bathing suit, a hopeful motor-listener, incessant wisher, — which issue of myself was my favorite? I better close my eyes & turn this into a story:

Story

Hair on top of my head, I'm dressed prim & serious, radiant, & focused on a test tube in my right hand. With my left I heat the beaker. The liquid inside foams up warm — golden & viscous like albumen: It's my Elixir, distilling in the middle of the night & preparing the sacrifice. A rather good sized man lies before me (is he a corpse?) I'm so serious in the room Liz is afraid to enter, even that her nervous stance or uneven breath may interfere. Dr. Aveshya now lowers an eyedropper of the hot potion into the man's mouth. (She is holding open his lips & depressing his tongue. "Don't worry," she says, hushed. He dreams a dream she had when she was a teenager: tires, a basement, some kind of pump. He feels something slip. She remembers he's in the future now, it's different. An old pain got up & quietly left out the back door while he was resting. A bird wakes him up again, he's confused & doesn't understand all these shifts: He's inside her mind now & he's beginning to understand. Another door opens & the air smells fresh. He glimpses her running outside, hears her tittering behind him, behind a tapestry. Memories flood in now & cracks are melting. She hugs him with all her allness & he lets himself give in, deep in his belly, he gives in to his body. He bends & sways & begins to let himself sob. "Quiet little sobs" she reminds. She's petting him gently & whispering to him softly & massaging one cruel sharp place with the tip of her silver knife. (She reminds him it will hurt to reverse the history, to give in to the love of the mamma. She's been too easy on him, she's a wimp for a teacher, but not any longer. Cruel Kali, Scary Lix. Open beauty open to chaos. Daring the power, patient, teacher.... "May I mold you," she asks with a sneering show of politeness & no lift in her voice. Of course she will try. Chin in, shoulders back. Stand & show me your tallness. "I require at least two things in a slave." She'd never seen the sheen of his shoulders before. (She dares herself to *go there*, into the sickness.) "Take off your shirt, so I can examine your nipples," she demands. She's a horny slut any way you look at it, the generic voice comments. (Is this language or is it a dairy? All crazies have their vocabulary, the straight man tried. Shut up & watch the movie, she reminded them.) Show me your dick, NOW, she challenges. He rushes to it & she approves with her eyebrows. Fuck the publisher, she declares, to hell with propriety. She "examines" that shaft ever so slowly, delighting in the newness, as usual, looking it over by taste & by lip pressure, so disgustingly sure of herself & all the more lushessly smug with each rise of their mutual pleasure created solely for her. And she holds the lead for hours as a tease in itself, maybe days before she lets herself swoon, saving up the pleasure. (She gave up her peach in the bedroom for a sack full of apples from around the stat.) Sneaking off to the orchard again, remembering arm in arm with her new catch, feeling his arm muscle with her other hand, breathing in excitement with the night air. (They each worry about her safety or her sanity, until slapped for subordination.) She points to a dead man hanging from an apple branch & warns with her sneer. He asked me to kill him, she tells, he couldn't stand the sight of me but couldn't stop looking & couldn't stand the pain. I'll teach you about wanting, she offered. It's a form of pain. None of us can have what we want, really: You eat your fruitcake, she's gone forever. I'm not driving you away, I'm opening me up.

ØØØØØØØØØØØØØØØØØØØØØØ

Language

Free at last her secret voice exclaims at the realization of sleep. "Let go of the rope, & out pops the tether." (Let the words fly out of the bowl.) The publisher's getting impatient: she lets the calendar enter the picture frame, then the story: Fear. Fear of the whole picture, fear to feel — she diagnoses his condition & massages him to sleep. If she was enlightened enough herself her behavior might dress her up & out the door, the sexy cynic gets her bit in, & now takes hold. I sink my teeth & purse my lips so darkly as to suck the air out of his cheeks when he bites my neck. (How dare she mix pornography with language writing?) Precious few of us know what it is to tease such limits, let alone why. My ever-inward spiraling inner understandings require new tools beyond parentheses & brackets. How paltry the pallet of the english language, how

few realize the shame of it. We who do need say "I'll shut up" & sing the night away. Sing the sounds of sound itself, which is far less polite than your mother might like.
Close the book & watch the head clear back to itself & then into the clouds disappears the one who opens the book to write the crystalline thought. "Concentrate," said the black man right before the slow turkish music came on. Oy, could I write a story."

Language:
Out of sheer loneliness one might, one night, write a lover into existence. Or consecrate an existing soft spot. I watch deep love take me over from inside and out, consumed or consuming me to desire to devour, to obsess & rob me of my own. It's my desire to own, to have to hold & grasp after, reach out & take. I see him there & I know the future but other's fear (& others' fear) make me put my dark glasses on & make believe. Nyx brings me a dripping wet young panther, as black as midnight & feeling all depth of suffering love. That's the all I can say in print, because the publisher's getting nervous & so is the author's husband. As you read. As I speak. (I write myself into existing existence, using parentheses as often as possible not as asides but as intos. INTO, she capitalizes on inner growth, she tweaks pain, words, & the boys' nipples. It's about DANGER, she remembers she could have worded it that way to the boy when he thought intensity so simply equated with ecstasy. "You left out the black," she chided: "Practice harder." Everything's so sexual now, she whispers to herself, but that's too easy. Rub my back, or chicken butt. (And I haven't lost track of the other. (End parentheses.)

‡‡‡‡‡‡‡‡‡‡‡‡‡‡‡‡‡‡‡‡‡‡‡‡‡‡‡‡‡‡‡‡

Diary

Circumspection irks us. We notice everything & in so doing we miss the tune of the boat. (Flies buzz themselves to death in my hair, while my husband lies frozen drunk next door.) Darkness is sarcastic. The publisher called a week too late: does he care why we write? "I'm writing myself into obsidian" —— there's a quote to revive her. I want her minus the urgent need; I need him to want me; I want him not to need me quite so much. We specialize in the unpublishable: stilted electronics, items separated only by commas, & boyscouts with cookies. Language dressed up and ever on the move. Every lines' other notated & upright or cut out of the sentence. "Chop-chop" with which my mother hurried me compared to him telling me, "Mama, trains don't really go 'choo-choo.'" Don't hold my breath to hear his spoken words. Breathe, instead, to match his patience. Delve into an isometric universe....

Victoria & Melampus

(1991)

Years ago, a luscious princess named Victoria, who all her life had had her cake & eaten it too, was on her usual walk one day looking for more & different cakes to try when before she knew it she found herself in a familiar new land, being led there willingly by a fascinating café goatboy. His name was Melampus, & with him she came alive to herself in so many new & familiar ways that for a short time she forgot all about cakes. Instead, she remembered about painting, writing, yoga, astrology, magic, ritual, taste, reading, &, most scrumptiously, music.

She'd been trained as a young girl by the finest court musicians. She showed much promise, but secretly detested the formality & fanfare of the music. Having no alternative available, she'd quit playing altogether before the age of ten.

Victoria & Melampus spent more than half of the riches she took with her when she split the palace on strange & beautiful musical instruments — crumpets, serpent horns, contrabassoon, dolzaina, fagotto, etc.. The two painted their bodies, donned big odd headresses & elfish shoes, & began a tour of the countryside with their unique show. The tiny villages they stopped in treated them like bizarre dignitaries from another planet, amused & intrigued.

Victoria herself on numerous occasions became intrigued, too, — with village men she eyed during their performances. She'd visit them after the show, returning early in the morning to help Melampus pack. His new sullenness annoyed her. Thoughts of all the new men distracted her. The terrain they were traveling got rougher, & she began to long for her old life. But their music was increasingly tighter, higher, wilder, more satisfying: she was addicted to it, couldn't do without it. She had to follow it, she had to stay with him.

Melampus withstood her continued nightly forays with a quiet stoicism & patience, assuming some day she'd grow out of it. Years went by. They stopped traveling, took a house in town & set up a fabulous gallery café theatre boarding house called "The Nervous Turtle." The Turtle attracted touring artists & musicians from all directions near & far & Victoria, who now called herself VaVa, fucked them all.

One evening, in passion play with a Russian sweetheart, she caught Melampus watching through the window. This in itself didn't shock her; she knew well of his voyeurist tendencies: What startled her were the horns poking out behind his ears, & the alternately pathetic & diabolical look on his face. It touched a dark place deep inside of her, but it would be years till she shook that part of herself free.

VaVa & Melampus had three children, each more unique & brilliant than the last, & The Turtle ran full swing all night for years, with the help of their many friends. VaVa had grown quite large & buxom, so sexy she was like a giant mango juicy & overripe. Melampus' horns were by now manifest in daylight as well as night, & fur had formed on each of their bodies - hers black velvety with gold flashes in cobalt shadow, his warm thick goat fur with cloven feet. VaVa, who had only become more voluptuous & more voracious with age, nonetheless abandoned her notorious promiscuity after the birth of their last son. By the time he was old enough to help run The Turtle, VaVa & Melampus found an abandoned farm outside of town & spent their last 35 years there, more or less removed from the hubbub they had been used to.

For miles wide & into other lands Melampus & VaVa, The Turtle, & their family were a legend. Crazy stories about them, some true & some invented, were repeated by mouth, recorded by hand. One of these stories was written by Melanie Celestial, the granddaughter of one of the couple's oldest & closest friends, about a visit to their farm. Dedicated to her lover, Hercules Infexius, it was published in a San Francisco sex journal just before the turn of the new century, & is reprinted here with permission of the author.

Just before dawn, sleeping in a loft space Melampus had built in the barn, I was awakened one night by hair-raising moans, cackles, caws, snorts, & long wailing sighs. A strong strange smoky smell was filling my ears & throat, enticing me out of the barn & into the dark. Just inside the woods was a new fire pit: VaVa's mad face was there in flames, in ecstasy. She was tied elaborately, mathematically wound in three colors of wire, her tits pressed inward against what looked like an ice cold filing cabinet wall. Was I in a room or out in the woods? I felt I must be dreaming. Pairs of Melampus' eyes flashed everywhere around me like lightning, no other sign of his body, except in the periphery of my vision a rapid penis in a disembodied hand.

A cold draft rubbed my shoulder. I turned around to just catch the glimpse of a black panther. The barn door had come open; I reached to close it, but instead I went out further into the dark night air. I glimpsed her again. A big chain was tugging her choker, struggling to slow her down. In her mouth was a magnificent bloody penis. Her gold eyes twinkled. A low purr rumbled in the woods, under my feet, now rattling my skull, an all-consuming vibration. I quick stuck my fingers in my vagina, as if plugging it up would stop the sound. It only changed it into a more satisfying hum, quieter & higher pitched, richer & sweeter the more I caressed myself.

I pricked my right nipple, pinching with fingernails to feel hot bolts of electricity shooting outwards from my aureole. I quick pricked the left too, & felt my center melt inside its core, heat rising up my belly from twat to navel, just beginning to heat the vast cauldron of elixir, sweet & slimy huge volume of liquid brewing now noisily, later bubbling, waiting to spray out, flow downwards, rivers of my wet come drenching my boots.

We're in the woods together now, Hercules, I'm stalking the panther to steal that cock from her, or was it an animal horn in her mouth? I want it badly, I'm out of my mind. You bumble behind me, burdened by the enormity of your erection. I drag you by it, I'm hot for the panther, I'm hot for VaVa. My breath is fire on you. I've got to bite, chew, devour, find the nearest tree trunk to fuck. I'm growling now, watching you rub my oversensed clit along the cold hard ground. The twigs scratch & wound me, my butt sticks way up because the tail is taking it. My tail whips you from behind, slapping your face for sniffing so close. "Lick my crack," I command & you love teasing me, licking it up the crack with slow thick wet tongue. Again I demand, with longer moans this time: "Eat me, devour me, you lovely wimp!" But just when you're getting into it I sense the panther lurking out there, off in the dark. I clamber up to my feet, knocking you down, ignoring your shining, your begging me not to go.

I've forgotten you, I'm off to find her. I leave you behind ruthlessly, sniffing into the woods, my sexy tail whipping curvaceously from side to side, on the prowl again. The thought that I actually might not return is too much for you. "Will she even turn back & glance at me?" You can barely glimpse me now but in between your moaning you hear me growl & hiss like cats in the night. Then it turns to wild frightful screeching so you pump your meat like mad feeling it rise & rise within you. Suddenly a shadow passes over you & you lose it, luscious lasting hell-fire of sex climbing up your being from the lowest deep down melting bedrock up & up melting through your abdomen, filling your ribs tingling you chest hairs, opening your shoulders, emptying your brain with flashing shockwaves of crackling explosions, lifting you off the forest floor out into the starry sky where you merge with the goddess of the night...You're nothing & everything, surrender fulfilled, complete with exhaustion, you fall asleep & dream of VaVa fucking an orange leopard in a sea of butter.

formula for labor

(1987)

try acerbic nimrod, acid scene, wire measles,   am law ticketed p,

Fuck

eben tempo,

zanthu-pointed gad

practically thick cupboard

A u s c h w i t z

kudzu,   PMT,   nations

WHYPOINT
tic cease

timber siberia   gland-ice   sabbatical timbersucker

ransack rape nonnybin smiles

muggenfuppy
pudges

Autumnprince, naphtha cetic

could put the case cold within it ma

diaperman
litaesthi-eeb

pummeled esthete:
sarco

Ainsi,
limerick mocked

rue-ha-ha

clipped or cupid, shrink
nympho

CUMIN ROBOT
Madcam Rabbi Kerchief, nan-point

SMINGE, CUCKOO
Nehru Tmesla Duke Obsiddian Nan-Point, rhu-ha

tismab pusillage,
al popped me te cornbin F.M.,

LIWAZARD

sybl, siberyl
pat acid gagged acidigene cuspidmucid
Yhev-cadet t m

tax-exempt

argued lowner

bookosser

anagramatic a-z poems for madison

(2002)

september 2002

My
Anartist
Debut
Is
Still
Opening,
Nascent

Wisconsin?
I
Savor
Cows
Over
Nightlife:
Southwesterly
I
Nest

Wistful
Intermediatist
Liz Was
(Lyx Ish)
Imagines
interests —
Jumping knowingly
Lessons multi-layered.

No one obfuscating the power of
Quizzing Reality.
Sisters, tenants,
Universitarians.
Variations on wealth, exercise, and
Yuppie zucchini.

Arboretum bicycle-stands.
Councilwomen deserving embraces.
Feminine guys.
Housing improved!
Johnson Street.
Kites-on-icicles.
Liz and Miekal
Newsworthy Onions
Parking questionable
Railroad tracks, sushi taverns.
The Universe at Vinny's.
Weeding.
Exclaiming
Yes! — Zipperer.

EVERY LINES OTHER by Elizabeth Was
Printed in the Autonomous Republic of Qazingulaza

www.ingramcontent.com/pod-product-compliance
Lightning Source LLC
LaVergne TN
LVHW041255080426
835510LV00009B/747